CHILDREN'S FICTION INDEX 7TH EDITION

Compiled by

Jennifer Madden and Margaret Hobson

Newcastle-Under-Lyme
A.A.L. Publishing

The Association of Assistant Librarians
(Group of the Library Association)
acknowledge the assistance of REMPLOY
in the production of this publication

1993

A CIP record for this book is
available from the British Library

ISBN 0–900092–85–8

Printed in Great Britain by Page Bros, Norwich

INTRODUCTION

This index has been compiled from children's fiction current at the date of going to press. Some out-of-print material has been included where it was felt it may be easily obtainable, but anything published before 1980 and out-of-print has been excluded. The index does not include picture books for the under-fives as these are indexed in a separate volume, although some books in picture-book format for older readers have been included. Also excluded are what were considered to be "genres" rather than subjects, e.g. "ghost stories", "science fiction", etc.

ACKNOWLEDGEMENTS

The authors wish to express their thanks to Messrs Woodfield and Stanley, Library Suppliers, of Huddersfield, and to Kirklees Cultural Services for unlimited access to their respective stocks.

ARRANGEMENT

Headings are as specific as possible because it was felt it would be easier to use the index, in spite of the resulting disadvantage of related headings being separated. "See" and "See also" headings are used to help overcome this. The main exception to this rule is "CONSERVATION AND POLLUTION", where specific headings would have resulted in a series of single entry headings. If there are a number of titles on one subject by one author, a generic series entry has been used in preference to listing all the titles. Publishers have been omitted as they were not thought useful, but dates of publication are given. Headings are arranged alphabetically. A letter is used to represent the age group for which the title is thought to be suitable:-

A = 0–5
B = 5–7
C = 7–9
D = 9–11
E = 12+

Two or more letters – A/B – denote an overlap.

AARDVARKS

TOMLINSON, Jill
Aardvark Who Wasn't Sure.(C) 1991 (ip)

ABANDONED CHILDREN

BAWDEN, Nina
Finding.(D) 1985 (ip)
DARKE, Marjorie
Come-back.(E) 1988 (ip)
FOX, Paula
Monkey Island.(D/E) 1992 (ip)
MACLACHLAN, Patricia
Journey.(D) 1992 (ip)
STRACHAN, Ian
Throwaways.(D/E) 1992 (ip)
THOMAS, Ruth
Secret.(D) 1990 (ip)

ABDUCTION See KIDNAPPING

ABORIGINAL FOLKTALES

TREZISE, Percy
Black Duck and Water Rat.(B/C) 1989 (ip)
Flying Fox Warriors.(B/C) 1989 (ip)
Gidja the Moon.(B/C) 1989 (ip)
Tarranmulli the Giant Quirkin.(B/C) 1989 (ip)

ABORIGINES

BERNDT, Catherine
Land of the Rainbow Snake.(E) 1980 (op)
MARSHALL, James Vance
Walkabout.(D/E) 1977 (ip)
WRIGHTSON, Patricia
Balyet.(E) 1989 (ip)
Nargun and the Stars.(E) 1973 (ip)

ACTING See also TRAVELLING PLAYERS

AKRILL, Caroline
Make Me a Star.(E) 1988 (op)
BILLINGTON, Rachel
Star Time.(D) 1984 (ip)
CATE, Dick
Alexander and the Star Part.(D) 1989 (op)
CROSS, Gillian
Wolf.(E) 1992 (ip)
DENISON, Mary
At Madam Muriel's.(E) 1979 (ip)
DRAZIN, Judith
Stage Fever.(D) 1983 (ip)
GERAS, Adele
Happy Endings.(E) 1988 (op)
HAMPSHIRE, Susan
Lucy Jane on Television.(D) 1989 (ip)
HARDCASTLE, Michael
James and the TV Star.(C) 1986 (ip)
HARRIS, Carmen
Naomi's Secret.(C) 1990 (ip)
HAYES, Sheila
No Autographs Please.(D/E) 1984 (ip)
LILLINGTON, Kenneth
Gabrielle D/E 1990 (ip)
POTTER, Maureen
Theatre Cat.(C) 1986 (ip)
RICHARDSON, Jean
Stage Struck.(D/E) 1991 (ip)
STREATFEILD, Noel
Curtain Up.(E) 1983 (ip)
Gemma.(E) 1968 (ip)
Gemma alone.(E) 1969 (ip)
Goodbye Gemma.(E) 1969 (ip)
TAYLOR, William
Break a Leg.(D/E) 1990 (ip)

URE, Jean
  Megastar.(D) 1986 (ip)
  Swings and Roundabouts.(D/E) 1988
  (ip)

ADDICTION See SPECIFIC ADDICTIONS

ADOLESCENCE

ADLER, C.S.
  Binding Ties.(E) 1988 (op)
ASHLEY, Bernard
  Bad Blood.(E) 1989 (ip)
BAWDEN, Nina
  Outside Child.(E) 1989 (ip)
BLUME, Judy
  Are You There God? It's Me, Margaret.(E) 1978 (ip)
  Forever.(E) 1976 (ip)
  Otherwise Known as Sheila the Great.(E) 1979 (ip)
  Then Again, Maybe I Won't.(E) 1979 (ip)
BOSSE, Malcolm J.
  Ganesh.(E) 1990 (ip)
BUSSELLE, Rebecca
  Bathing Ugly.(E) 1990 (op)
BYARS, Betsy
  Burning Questions of Bingo Brown.(E) 1988 (ip)
  Cybil War.(E) 1983 (ip)
CHRISTIE, Sally
  Not Just Jemima.(E) 1990 (ip)
CORMIER, Robert
  Darcy.(E) 1991 (ip)
DALE, Mitzi
  Round the Bend.(E) 1990 (op)
DAY, David
  Are You Listening, Karen?.(E) 1983 (ip)
HANNAM, Charles
  Almost an Englishman.(E) 1979 (ip)
KAYE, Geraldine
  Comfort Herself.(C) 1984 (ip)
KENNEMORE, Tim
  Middle of the Sandwich.(D) 1981 (ip)
MARSHALL, Heather
  Gemma, Brooke and Madeleine.(E) 1989 (op)

ADOPTION AND FOSTERING

ASHLEY, Bernard
  Trouble with Donovan Croft.(D/E) 1980 (ip)
BAWDEN, Nina
  Finding.(E) 1985 (ip)
BERESFORD, Elisabeth
  One of the Family.(D) 1985 (op)
BYARS, Betsy
  Pinballs.(E) 1992 (ip)
DUNLOP, Eileen
  Fox Farm.(D/E) 1978 (ip)
HOLLAND, Isabel
  House in the Woods.(E) 1991 (ip)
HUNT, Pauline
  Red Pepper.(E) 1983 (ip)
JACOBS, Barbara
  Stick.(D) 1990 (ip)
LOWRY, Lois
  Find a Stranger, Say Goodbye.(E) 1988 (ip)
MORPURGO, Michael
  Little Foxes.(D) 1990 (ip)
NEWMAN, Marjorie
  Michael and the Jumble Sale Cat.(C) 1990 (ip)
PATERSON, Katherine
  Great Gilly Hopkins.(E) 1981 (ip)
SPENCE, Eleanor
  Left Overs.(D) 1982 (ip)
WILSON, Jacqueline
  Story of Tracy Beaker.(D) 1991 (ip)

AEROPLANES

HAMLEY, Dennis
  Fourth Plane at the Flypast.(E) 1985 (ip)
  Landings.(E) 1981 (op)
MARK, Jan
  Thunder and Lightnings.(D/E) 1978 (ip)
PEYTON, Kathleen M.
  Edge of the Cloud.(E) 1969 (ip)

AFRICA

JENKINS, A.C.
  Ghost Elephant.(D) 1981 (ip)

AFRICA – FOLK TALES See also ASHANTI – FOLK TALES

COURLANDER, Harold
  Crest and the Hide.(E) 1984 (op)
FAIRMAN, Tony
  Bury My Bones But Keep My
  Words.(D/E) 1991 (ip)
GREAVES, Nick
  When Hippo was Hairy.(D/E) 1990
  (ip)
PITCHER, Diana
  Mischief Maker: African Tales of
  Nogwaya the Hare.(D/E) 1984 (op)

AFRICA – MYTHS AND LEGENDS

COURLANDER, Harold
  Crest and the Hide.(E) 1984 (op)
KNAPPERT, Jan
  Fables from Africa.(C/D) 1981 (ip)
  Kings, Gods and Spirits from African
  Mythology.(E) 1986 (ip)

ALASKA

CALVERT, Patricia
  Hour of the Wolf.(D/E) 1983 (ip)

ALCOHOL ADDICTION

HOLLAND, Isabel
  House in the Woods.(E) 1991 (ip)
TAYLOR, Willia
  Paradise Lane.(E) 1987 (ip)

ALIENS

ALCOCK, Vivien
  Thing in the Woods.(C) 1989 (ip)
BAKER, Pip
  Watt on Earth.(D) 1991 (ip)
BALL, Brian
  Truant from Space.(C) 1988 (ip)
FAVILLE, Barry
  Return.(D) 1989 (ip)
FISK, Nicholas
  Broops! Down the Chimney.(D) 1991
  (ip)
  Trillions.(D) 1973 (ip)
FREEMAN, Maggie
  Danger! Space Pirates.(D) 1987 (op)
LAVELLE, Sheila
  Copycat.(C) 1989 (ip)
  Spots in Space.(C) 1988 (ip)
  Topsy-turvy Teacher.(C) 1988 (ip)
LIMB, Sue
  China Lee.(D) 1987 (ip)

MAHY, Margaret
  Alien in the Family.(D) 1986 (ip)
NASH, Margaret
  Over the Moon and Far Away.(C)
  1988 (ip)
RODGERS, Frank
  Summertime Christmas Present.(C)
  1989 (ip)
SCHOCH, Tim
  Creeps: An Alien in Our School(D)
  1987 (ip)
SHELDON, Dyan
  Harry and Chicken.(C) 1990 (ip)
  Harry the Explorer.(C) 1991 (ip)
STRONG, Jeremy
  Woff.(C) 1983 (ip)
SWINDELLS, Robert
  Postbox Mystery.(C) 1988 (ip)
THOMSON, Pat
  Strange Exchange.(D/E) 1991 (ip)
TULLY, John
  Slade.(D) 1985 (ip)
WRIGHT, Ralph
  Angela's Aliens.(D) 1991 (ip)

ALPHABETS

KING, Clive
  Twenty Two Letters.(D/E) 1966 (ip)

AMERICA See UNITED STATES OF AMERICA

AMERICAN CIVIL WAR

CRANE, Stephen
  Red Badge of Courage.(E) 1992 (ip)

AMERICAN FOOTBALL

JAMES, Laurence
  End Zone.(E) 1989 (op)
  First and Ten.(E) 1988 (op)
  Running Back.(E) 1988 (op)
  Second and Five.(E) 1988 (op)
  Third and Goal.(E) 1987 (ip)
  Touch Down.(E) 1987 (ip)

AMERICAN INDIANS See NATIVE AMERICANS

AMERICAN WEST

BERESFORD, Elisabeth
  Wooden Gun.(E) 1989 (ip)
COREN, Alan
  Lone Arthur.(D) 1976 (ip)
DEARY, Terry
  Bad Bart and Billy the Brave.(C) 1989
  (ip)
  Treasure of Crazy Horse.(C) 1990 (ip)
DARKE, Marjorie
  Rainbow Sandwich.(C) 1990 (ip)
FISK, Nicholas
  Backlash.(D) 1988 (ip)
FLEISCHMAN, Sid
  Man on the Moon-eyed Horse.(C)
  1980 (ip)
HAHN, Mary Downing
  Wait Till Helen Comes.(D/E) 1990
  (ip)
LANE, Rose Wilder
  Let the Hurricane Roar(D/E 1982 (ip)
WADDELL, Martin
  Little Obie and the Kidnap.(C/D)
  1991 (ip)
WILSON, Jacqueline
  This Girl.(E) 1988 (ip)

AMISH

SMUCKER, Barbara Claassen
  Amish Adventure.(D) 1984 (ip)

AMPUTATION

VOIGT, Cynthia
  Izzy, Willy-nilly.(E) 1987 (ip)

ANANSI See WEST INDIES – FOLK TALES

ANCIENT EGYPT See also EGYPT

HARRIS, Rosemary
  Bright and Morning Star.(E) 1972 (ip)
  Moon in the Cloud.(E) 1989 (ip)
  Shadow on the Sun.(E) 1989 (ip)
POND, Roy
  Pyramid Voyagers.(D) 1992 (ip)
  Tomb Travellers.(D) 1992 (ip)
TURNBULL, Ann
  Queen Cat.(C) 1989 (ip)

ANCIENT EGYPT – MYTHS AND LEGENDS

GREEN, Roger Lancelyn
  Tales of Ancient Egypt.(D) 1989 (ip)

ANCIENT GREECE See also GREECE

SMITH, Joan
  Apollo's Child.(E) 1989 (ip)

ANCIENT GREECE – MYTHS AND LEGENDS

GARFIELD, Leon
  God beneath the Sea.(D/E) 1991 (ip)
  Golden Shadow.(E) 1991 (ip)
GREEN, Roger Lancelyn
  Luck of Troy.(D/E) 1990 (ip)
  Tales of the Greek Heroes.(D) 1989
  (ip)
OLDFIELD, Pamela
  Stories from Ancient Greece.(C) 1988
  (ip)
ROBINSON, Tony
  Odysseus.(D) 1986 (ip)

ANCIENT ROME See also ROME

ROBERTSON, Jenny
  Branded!(E) 1991 (ip)
SUTCLIFF, Rosemary
  Mark of the Horse Lord.(D/E) 1983
  (ip)

ANGELS

WADDELL, Martin
  Fred the Angel.(C) 1989 (ip)
WILLIAMS, Ursula Moray
  Bellabelinda and the No-good
  Angel.(D) 1982 (ip)

ANIMAL RESCUE

BERESFORD, Elisabeth
  Animals Nobody Wanted.(D) 1982
  (ip)
CLEVELAND-PECK, Patricia
  Ark Angel.(C) 1991 (ip)
CROSS, Gillian
  Rescuing Gloria (op).(D) 1989
PEYTON, Kathleen M.
  Poor Badger.(C) 1990 (ip)
POLLEN, Pandora
  Moonstruck Mongrel.(D) 1989 (ip)

ANIMAL RIGHTS

BOSTON, Lucy M.
  Stranger at Green Knowe.(D) 1961 (ip)
DANN, Colin
  Great Escape.(D/E) 1990 (ip)
GREAVES, Margaret
  Juniper's Journey.(C) 1990 (ip)
MORPURGO, Michael
  When the Whales Came.(D/E) 1990 (ip)
NEWBERY, Linda
  Run with the Hare.(E) 1988 (ip)
PEYTON, Kathleen M.
  Poor Badger.(C/D) 1990 (ip)
TAYLOR, Theodore
  Sniper.(E) 1991 (ip)
WESLEY, Mary
  Speaking Terms.(D) 1992 (ip)
WESTALL, Robert
  If Cats Could Fly.(C) 1990 (ip)

ANIMALS See also INDIVIDUAL SPECIES

ANIMAL
  Animal Tales from "Listen with Mother".(B) 1984 (ip)
BERESFORD, Elisabeth
  Charlie's Ark.(C) 1989 (ip)
HEWETT, Anita
  Puffin Book of Animal Stories.(C) 1972 (ip)
KEMP, Gene
  Dog Days and Cat Naps.(D) 1983 (ip)
LIVELY, Penelope
  Voyage of QV66.(D) 1978 (ip)
MANNING-SANDERS, Ruth
  Animal Stories.(C/D) 1980 (ip)
O'MARA, Lesley
  Book of Animal Stories.(D) 1989 (ip)
STEWART, Paul
  Adam's Ark.(D/E) 1990 (ip)

ANOREXIA NERVOSA

HAUTZIG, Deborah
  Second Star to the Right.(E) 1991 (ip)

ANTEATERS

STEELE, Mary Quintard
  Citizen Arkwright.(C/D) 1991 (ip)

APARTHEID

JONES, Toeckey
  Skin Deep.(E) 1985 (ip)
NAIDOO, Beverley
  Chain of Fire.(D/E) 1989 (ip)
  Journey to Jo'burg: A South African Story.(D/E) 1987 (ip)
SILVER, Norman
  Eye for Colour.(E) 1991 (ip)
  No Tigers in Africa.(E) 1990 (ip)

APPRENTICES (EIGHTEENTH CENTURY)

GARFIELD, Leon
  Cloak.(D/E) 1976 (ip)
  Labour in Vain.(D/E) 1977 (ip)
  Mirror, Mirror.(D/E) 1976 (ip)
  Moss and Blister.(D/E) 1976 (ip)
  Tom Titmarsh's Devil.(D/E) 1977 (ip)

ARCHAEOLOGY

ROCK, Nora
  Monkey's Perfect.(D) 1978 (ip)
TREASE, Geoffrey
  Calabrian Quest.(E) 1990 (ip)
  Shadow under the Sea.(E) 1990 (ip)

ARMADA See SPANISH ARMADA

ARTHURIAN LEGEND See KING ARTHUR

ASHANTI FOLK TALES

APPIAH, Peggy
  Pineapple Child and Other Tales from the Ashanti.(D) 1989 (ip)
  Tales of an Ashanti Father.(D) 1987 (ip)
  Why the Hyena Does Not Care for Fish.(D) 1977 (ip)

ASIA See also INDIVIDUAL COUNTRIES

MORRIS, Jean
  Donkey's Crusade.(E) 1989 (op)

ASTHMA

THESMAN, Jean
  Appointment with a Stranger.(E) 1991 (ip)

5

YEATMAN, Linda
  Clare's Gymnastic Poodle: Story about Asthma.(C/D) 1990 (ip)

ATHLETICS See also INDIVIDUAL SPORTS

ALEXANDER, Barrie
  Ben Goes for Gold.(D/E) 1991 (ip)

AUSTRALIA See also ABORIGINES

ALINGTON, Gabriel
  Stars are Upside Down.(D/E) 1991 (ip)
BAILLIE, Allan
  Hero.(D/E) 1990 (ip)
  Riverman.(D/E) 1986 (ip)
BAKER, Ivy
  Monday Sheepdog.(E) 1987 (op)
BARNETT, Gillian
  Gumboots and Other Risks.(D) 1990 (ip)
BATES, Dianne
  Grandma Cadbury's Safari Tours.(D) 1990 (ip)
  Grandma Cadbury's Trucking Tales.(D) 1989 (ip)
BERNARD, Patricia
  Kangaroos Kids.(D) 1989 (ip)
BRINSMEAD, Hesba Fay
  Pastures of the Blue Crane.(E) 1978 (ip)
  Sand Forest.(E) 1986 (op)
BURTON, Hester
  No Beat of Drum.(D/E) 1987 (op)
CARR, Roger Vaughan
  Firestorm!(E) 1985 (ip)
GREEN, Cliff
  Further Adventures of Riverboat Bill.(D) 1981 (ip)
HILL, Deirdre
  Flight from Fear.(D/E) 1989 (ip)
MARSHALL, James Vance
  Walkabout.(E) 1977 (ip)
MATTINGLEY, Christobel
  New Patches for Old.(D/E) 1980 (op)
NOONAN, Michael
  McKenzie's Boots.(D/E) 1989 (ip)

O'NEILL, Judith
  Deepwater.(D/E) 1989 (op)
  Jess and the River Kids.(D/E) 1984 (ip)
  Stringybark Summer.(D/E) 1990 (ip)
SOUTHALL, Ivan
  Ash Road.(D/E) 1970 (ip)
  Hills End.(D/E) 1970 (ip)
STEELE, Mary Quintard
  Mallyroot's Pub at Misery Ponds.(C/D) 1988 (ip)
THOMPSON, Valerie
  Gold on the Wind.(D/E) 1977 (ip)
TURNER, Ethel
  Family at Misrule.(D/E) 1989 (op)
  Seven Little Australians.(D/E) 1989 (ip)
WHEATLEY, Nadia
  Blooding.(E) 1987 (ip)
WRIGHTSON, Patricia
  Moondark.(D/E) 1986 (ip)

AUSTRALIAN ABORIGINES See ABORIGINES

AVALANCHES

BAUDET, Stephanie
  Avalanche.(C) 1986 (op)
LOEFF, A.Rutgers Van Der
  Avalanche.(D/E) 1971 (ip)

BABIES

MENEZES, Anne De
  Orange Cake for Tea.(C) 1990 (ip)
REUTERSWARD, Maud
  Noah is My Name.(B/C) 1991 (ip)
ROGERS, Paul
  Amazing Babies.(C) 1990 (ip)

BADGER BAITING

MASTERS, Anthony
  Badger.(E) 1988 (ip)

BADGERS

BURKETT, Molly
  Year of the Badger.(D) 1985 (ip)
STRANGER, Joyce
  Honeywell Badger.(D) 1986 (ip)

BALI – FOLK TALES

COX, David
Ayu and the Perfect Moon.(B) 1984 (op)

BALLET

ASHER, Sandy
Just Like Jenny.(D/E) 1982 (ip)
BALL, Brian
Bella at the Ballet.(B) 1990 (ip)
ESTORIL, Jean
Drina series.(D/E) 1970 (ip)
HAMPSHIRE, Susan
Lucy Jane and the Dancing Competition.(D) 1991 (ip)
Lucy Jane at the Ballet.(D) 1989 (ip)
RICHARDSON, Jean
Dancer in the Wings.(D/E) 1985 (op)
First Step.(D/E) 1984 (op)
One Foot on the Ground.(D/E) 1986 (op)
STREATFEILD, Noel
Ballet Shoes.(E) 1970 (ip)
Ballet Shoes for Anna.(E) 1972 (ip)
URE, Jean
Hi There, Supermouse!(E) 1985 (ip)
Nicola Mimosa.(E) 1985 (ip)
Proper Little Nooryeff.(E) 1982 (ip)

BARGES See CANALS

BASEBALL

SMITH, Robert Kimmel
Bobby Baseball.(D) 1990 (op)

BASILISK

LYONS, Greg
Lonely Basilisk.(B) 1989 (ip)

BASKETBALL

JAMES, Laurence
Grand Slam.(E) 1988 (ip)
Home Run.(E) 1988 (ip)
Outside Shot.(D/E) 1989 (op)

BATS

ALLEN, Eleanor
Max and the Birthday Bat.(C) 1987 (op)
ROGERS, Paul
Bat Boy.(D) 1991 (ip)

TURNBULL, Ann
Trouble with Bats.(C) 1990 (ip)

BEARS

CORBETT, W.J.
Bear Who Stood on His Head.(C) 1988 (ip)
DICKINSON, Peter
Dancing Bear.(E) 1985 (ip)
JOHNS, Eric
Three Bears Lend a Hand.(B) 1990 (ip)

BEES

KENEALLY, Thomas
Ned Kelly and the City of the Bees.(C/D) 1978 (ip)
NEEDLE, Jan
Bee Rustlers.(D) 1980 (ip)
OWSIANKA, Maria
Legend of the Hive.(D) 1988 (ip)

BELFAST See NORTHERN IRELAND

BEOWULF

SUTCLIFF, Rosemary
Dragon Slayer: Story of Beowulf.(D) 1970 (ip)

BERLIN WALL

LUTZEIER, Elizabeth
Wall.(E) 1991 (ip)

BICYCLES See also CYCLE RACING

GILES, Barbara
Flying Backwards.(D) 1985 (ip)
HACKLES, Lynn
Racing Start.(D/E) 1991 (ip)
LLOYD, Errol
Sasha and the Bicycle Thieves.(C) 1988 (ip)
POWLING, Chris
Mustang Machine.(D) 1983 (op)
ROGERS, Paul
Boneshaker.(C) 1989 (ip)
SMITH, Alexander McCall
Ice-cream Bicycle.(B/C) 1990 (ip)

WILMER, Diane
  Bike Run.(D/E) 1987 (ip)

BIRDS See also INDIVIDUAL SPECIES

ALLEN, Judy
  Something Rare and Special.(E) 1989 (ip)
MORPURGO, Michael
  Colly's Barn.(C) 1991 (ip)
PHIPSON, Joan
  Bird Smuggler.(D) 1977 (ip)

BIRTHDAYS

FLEETWOOD, Jenni
  Happy Birthday: Nine Birthday Stories.(C) 1991 (ip)
GERAS, Adele
  Magic Birthday.(C) 1992 (ip)
HAWKINS, Elizabeth
  Henry's Most Unusual Birthday.(C) 1990 (ip)
MORGAN, Alison
  Biggest Birthday Card in the World.(C) 1989 (ip)
TAYLOR, Minna
  Awful Birthday Present.(B) 1991 (ip)

BLINDNESS

ALLAN, Mabel Esther
  View beyond My Father.(E) 1987 (ip)
COOKSON, Catherine
  Go Tell it to Mrs. Golightly.(D/E) 1989 (ip)
DICKINSON, Peter
  Annerton Pit.(E) 1977 (ip)
DOHERTY, Berlie
  Spellhorn.(D/E) 1989 (ip)
FINE, Anne
  Summer-house Loon.(E) 1978 (ip)
RHIND, Mary
  Dark Shadow.(E) 1989 (ip)
URE, Jean
  See You Thursday.(E) 1981 (ip)
WILDE, Nicholas
  Into the Dark.(E) 1989 (ip)

BOATS AND BOATING See also CANALS, SEA

PEARCE, Philippa
  Minnow on the Say.(D/E) 1974 (ip)

PEYTON, Kathleen M.
  Plan for Birdsmarsh.(D/E) 1980 (op)
RANSOME, Arthur
  Big Six.(D/E) 1940 (ip)
  Coot Club.(D/E) 1934 (ip)
  Great Northern?(D/E) 1947 (ip)
  Missee Lee.(D/E) 1941 (ip)
  Peter Duck.(D/E) 1968 (ip)
  Picts and Martyrs.(D/E) 1941 (ip)
  Pigeon Post.(D/E) 1969 (ip)
  Secret Water.(D/E) 1939 (ip)
  Swallowdale.(D/E) 1931 (ip)
  Swallows and Amazons.(D/E) 1930 (ip)
  We Didn't Mean to Go to Sea.(D/E) 1969 (ip)
  Winter Holiday.(D/E) 1933 (ip)
VOIGT, Cynthia
  Seventeen against the Dealer.(E) 1990 (ip)

BOER WAR

TANTON, Bruce
  Time's Lost Hero.(D) 1990 (ip)

BOGGARTS

MORSE, Brian
  TV Ghost.(C) 1991 (ip)

BOSTON TEA PARTY

FORBES, Esther
  Johnny Tremain.(E) 1989 (op)

BOXING

BALLARD, Martin
  Dockie.(E) 1983 (op)

BRAZIL

PUIG, Evelyn
  Chico, the Street Boy.(D) 1984 (ip)
VASCONCELOS, Jose Mauro De
  My Sweet-orange Tree.(D/E) 1983 (op)

BRER ANANSI See WEST INDIES – FOLK TALES

BRER RABBIT

LESTER, Julius
    Adventures of Brer Rabbit.(C) 1987
    (ip)

BRIDESMAIDS

COCKETT, Mary
    Bickering Bridesmaids.(C) 1991 (ip)
HOOPER, Mary
    Revolting Bridesmaid.(C) 1990 (ip)

BRITISH ISLES – FOLK TALES

CROSSLEY-HOLLAND, Kevin
    British and Irish Folk Tales.(D/E)
    1990 (ip)
GARNER, Alan
    Bag of Moonshine.(D/E) 1986 (ip)

BRONZE AGE

SUTCLIFF, Rosemary
    Warrior Scarlet.(D/E) 1976 (ip)

BROWNIES

GOWAR, Mick
    Brenda the Do-it-yourself
    Brownie.(C) 1992 (ip)
RICHARDSON, Dorothy
    Brownie Series.(C) 1985 (op)
SYKES, Pamela
    Brownies Series.(C) 1987 (op)

BRUNSWICK BAY

TOMLINSON, Theresa
    Flither Pickers.(D/E) 1990 (ip)

BULLS

GARDAM, Jane
    Kit.(C) 1983 (ip)

BULLYING

ALCOCK, Vivien
    Trial of Anna Cotman.(E) 1991 (ip)
ASHLEY, Bernard
    High Pavement Blues.(E) 1990 (ip)
CATE, Dick
    Foxcover.(D/E) 1989 (ip)
CHAMBERS, Aidan
    Present Takers.(D) 1987 (ip)
COPPARD-QUIRK, Yvonne
    Bully.(E) 1991 (ip)

CORMIER, Robert
    Beyond the Chocolate War.(E) 1985
    (ip)
    Chocolate War.(E) 1978 (ip)
JOHNS, Eric
    Jason and the School Bully.(C/D)
    1988 (ip)
KEMP, Gene
    Gowie Corby Plays Chicken.(D) 1979
    (ip)
LLOYD, Carole
    Speccy Four Eyes.(D) 1991 (ip)
NICHOLLS, Christopher
    Ziggurat.(E) 1991 (ip)
PEYTON, Kathleen M.
    Froggett's Revenge.(D) 1985 (ip)
POWLING, Chris
    Daredevils or Scaredycats.(D) 1981
    (ip)

BURMA – FOLK TALES

TROUGHTON, Joanna
    Believe It or Not.(B) 1991 (ip)

BYZANTIUM

DICKINSON, Peter
    Dancing Bear.(E) 1985 (ip)

CALVES See COWS

CAMELS

TATE, Joan
    Dad's Camel.(C) 1990 (ip)

CAMPING

LAMBERT, Thelma
    Benny's Night Out.(B) 1991 (ip)
LAVELLE, Sheila
    Ursula Camping.(C) 1986 (ip)

CANADA

HAMMOND, Ralph
    Black Gold on the Double
    Diamond.(E) 1953 (ip)
MAYNE, William
    Drift.(E) 1985 (ip)
RAYMOND, Patrick
    Maple Moon.(E) 1992 (ip)
ROBERTS, Charles G. D.
    Eyes of the Wilderness.(D/E) 1980
    (ip)

SMUCKER, Barbara Claassen
Days of Terror.(D/E) 1981 (op)
Jacob's Little Giant.(D) 1987 (ip)

CANALS

BARBER, Antonia
Ring in the Rough Stuff.(E) 1984 (op)
BARTON, P.
Last Run.(D/E) 1980 (ip)
CARPENTER, Humphrey
Joshers.(D/E) 1977 (ip)
CHANEY, Jill
Canary Yellow.(D) 1978 (ip)
JONES, Carol
Painted Boats.(D) 1979 (ip)
MAYNE, William
Gideon Ahoy!(D/E) 1987 (ip)
WAIN, John
Lizzie's Floating Shop.(E) 1986 (ip)

CANCER

ASHLEY, Bernard
Bad Blood.(E) 1987 (ip)
LITTLE, Jean
Mama's Going to Buy You a Mock-
ingbird.(D/E) 1986 (ip)
URE, Jean
One Green Leaf.(E) 1987 (ip)

CANDLES

LUNN, Janet
One Hundred Shining Candles.(B)
1991 (ip)

CANOEING

COLLINS, Janet
River's Revenge.(D/E) 1991 (ip)

CAREERS

PRICE, Susan
Sticks and Stones.(E) 1992 (ip)
WEBSTER, Joanne
Marigold Days.(E) 1985 (op)
WILLARD, Barbara
Family Tower.(E) 1988 (ip)

CARIBBEAN See WEST INDIES and INDIVIDUAL COUNTRIES

CARING

ASHLEY, Bernard
Bit of Give and Take.(C) 1986 (ip)

CARS

FISK, Nicholas
Talking Car.(C) 1990 (ip)
POWLING, Chris
ELF 61.(C) 1990 (ip)
WILLARD, Barbara
Family Tower.(E) 1988 (ip)

CARTOONS

BYARS, Betsy
Cartoonist.(D/E) 1981 (ip)

CASTLES

COCKETT, Mary
Cat and the Castle.(C) 1982 (op)

CATS

ARKLE, Phyllis
Railway Cat and Digby.(C) 1986 (ip)
Railway Cat and the Horse.(D) 1988
(ip)
Railway Cat's Secret.(C) 1987 (ip)
BRADMAN, Tony
Gary and the Magic Cat.(B) 1989 (ip)
BROWN, George Mackay
Six Lives of Fankle the Cat.(D) 1984
(ip)
CASTOR, Harriet
Fat Puss and Friends.(C) 1985 ip
COCKETT, Mary
Cat and the Castle.(C) 1982 (op)
Tracker.(C) 1984 (ip)
DANN, Colin
City Cats.(D) 1991 (ip)
King of the Vagabonds.(D/E) 1987
(ip)
FOX, Paula
One-eyed Cat.(E) 1985 (ip)
GRANGER, Michele
Summer House Cat.(D) 1990 (ip)
KING-SMITH, Dick
Martin's Mice.(C/D) 1988 (ip)
Mouse Butcher.(D) 1981 (ip)
LINDSAY, Gillian
Owl in Winter.(C) 1986 (ip)
LYTTON, Claire
Mr Jenkins the Cat.(D) 1987 (op)

MANGAN, Anne
  School Cat.(B) 1990 (ip)
MEYNELL, Laurence
  Smoky Joe in Trouble.(D) 1984 (ip)
PEARCE, Philippa
  Mrs Cockle's Cat.(C) 1988 (ip)
POTTER, Maureen
  Theatre Cat.(C) 1986 (ip)
PRICE, Susan
  Thunderpumps.(C) 1990 (ip)
ROSEN, Billi
  Sophie's Cat.(D) 1991 ip
SLEIGH, Barbara
  Carbonel.(D) 1970 (ip)
  Carbonel and Calidor.(D) 1980 (ip)
STOLZ, Mary
  Cat Walk.(C/D) 1985 (ip)
TOMLINSON, Jill
  Cat Who Wanted to Go Home.(C)
  1991 (ip)
TURNBULL, Ann
  Queen Cat.(C) 1989 (ip)
  Summer of the Cats.(C/D) 1987 (op)
WATTS, Marjorie-Ann
  Mill House Cat.(D) 1988 (ip)
WESTALL, Robert
  Blitzcat.(D/E) 1991 (ip)
  Walk on the Wild Side: Cat
  Stories.(D/E) 1989 (ip)
  Yaxley's Cat.(E) 1991 (ip)
WILSON, A.N.
  Stray.(D/E) 1987 (ip)
  Tabitha Stories.(C) 1990 (ip)
ZABEL, Jennifer
  Purr.(C) 1989 (ip)
  Wimbleball.(C) 1990 (ip)

CAVE PAINTINGS

DENZEL, Justin F.
  Boy of the Painted Cave.(E) 1988 (ip)

CAVES See also CAVE PAINTINGS

TREASE, Geoffrey
  Flight of Angels.(D) 1989 (op)

CELLO

MACLACHLAN, Patricia
  Facts and Fictions of Minna Pratt.(D)
  1991 (ip)

**CENTRAL AMERICA See
INDIVIDUAL COUNTRIES**

**CHANNEL ISLANDS See
INDIVIDUAL ISLANDS**

CHEATING

RUFFELL, Ann
  Computer Cheat.(D) 1987 (op)
SMITH, Alexander McCall
  Harriet Bean and the League of
  Cheats.(C) 1991 (ip)

CHEETAHS

CANNING, Victor
  Runaways.(E) 1973 (ip)
WESTALL, Robert
  Creature in the Dark.(C) 1988 (ip)

CHILDHOOD

KEMP, Gene
  Well.(C/D) 1988 (ip)
LINDGREN, Astrid
  Cherry Time at Bullerby.(C) 1991 (ip)
  Happy Days at Bullerby.(C) 1961 (ip)
  Six Bullerby Children.(C) 1991 (ip)
LIVELY, Penelope
  Going Back.(D) 1975 (ip)

CHILDREN IN INDUSTRY

ROBERTSON, Wendy
  Lizza.(E) 1988 (op)
WALSH, Jill Paton
  Chance Child.(D) 1978 (ip)

CHILDREN'S NANNY

WEBSTER, Joanne
  Marigold Days.(E) 1985 (op)

CHILDREN'S RIGHTS

DANZIGER, Paula
  Can You Sue Your Parents for Mal-
  practice?(E) 1986 (ip)
HARLEY, Rex
  Troublemaker.(E) 1991 (ip)

CHILE

WATSON, James
  Talking in Whispers.(E) 1983 (ip)

CHIMPANZEES

DICKINSON, Peter
  Eva.(E) 1988 (ip)
MORPURGO, Michael
  Mr Nobody's Eyes.(D/E) 1990 (ip)

CHINA

BAILLIE, Allan
  China Coin.(E) 1991 (ip)
BELL, William
  Forbidden City.(E) 1991 (ip)
DEJONG, Meindert
  House of Sixty Fathers.(D) 1971 (ip)
PATERSON, Katherine
  Rebels of the Heavenly Kingdom.(E)
  1983 (ip)

CHINA – FOLK TALES

LIYI HE
  Spring of Butterflies and Other
  Chinese Folk Tales.(D) 1985 (ip)

CHRISTMAS

ANDERSON, Rachel
  Happy Christmas, Little Angel.(D)
  1991 (ip)
BRAGG, Melvyn
  Christmas Child.(D) 1989 (ip)
CORRIN, Sara
  Round the Christmas Tree.(B/C) 1985
  (ip)
DELTON, Judy
  No Time for Christmas.(B) 1988 (ip)
GERAS, Adele
  Christmas Cat.(B) 1989 (ip)
  Nina's Magic.(C) 1990 (ip)
HILL, Susan
  Glass Angels.(C) 1991 (ip)
KAYE, Geraldine
  Donkey Christmas.(C) 1988 (ip)
KINGMAN, Lee
  Best Christmas.(C) 1986 (ip)
LUNN, Janet
  One Hundred Shining Candles.(B)
  1991 (ip)
MAYNE, William
  Rings on Her Fingers.(B/C) 1991 (ip)
OLDFIELD, Pamela
  Christmas Ghost.(C) 1985 (op)

PITCHER, Caroline
  Red-spotted Reindeer.(C) 1988 (op)
POWLING, Chris
  Phantom Carwash.(C) 1986 (ip)
RUFFELL, Ann
  Cathy's Christmas Project.(C) 1991
  (ip)
RYAN, Margaret
  Queen Bea's Christmas.(C) 1990 (ip)
RYLANT, Cynthia
  Silver Packages and Other
  Stories.(C/D) 1987 (ip)
SCOTT, Hugh
  Summertime Santa.(C) 1990 (ip)
STONBOROUGH, Margaret
  Father Christmas Trap.(C) 1988 (ip)
THEROUX, Paul
  Christmas Card.(C) 1979 (ip)
  London Snow.(C) 1979 (ip)
WILLIAMSON, Duncan
  Tell Me a Story for Christmas.(D)
  1987 (ip)
WILSON, Gina
  Polly Pipes Up.(C) 1989 (ip)
WOOD, Ann
  Child's Christmas.(B/C) 1988 (ip)

CINEMA See FILMS

CIRCUS

ALCOCK, Vivien
  Travellers by Night.(D) 1983 (ip)
JENNINGS, Eve
  Colonel Cornflake's Circus.(C) 1978
  (ip)
LOSCHUTZ, Gert
  Penny-mark: The Tale of Tom Cour-
  tey's Honour and Benjamin Walz's
  Shame.(D) 1990 (ip)
MORPURGO, Michael
  Mr Nobody's Eycs.(D/E) 1990 (ip)
STREATFEILD, Noel
  Circus is Coming.(E) 1970 (ip)

CITY FARMS

ALLEN, Judy
  Cheap Sheep Shock.(C) 1991 (ip)
  Dim Thin Ducks.(C) 1990 (ip)
  Great Pig Sprint.(C) 1990 (ip)
  Long-loan Llama.(C) 1991 (ip)

CITY LIFE

MACGIBBON, Jean
 Hal.(E) 1980 (ip)
MCNEILL, Janet
 Battle of St George Without.(D/E)
 1966 (ip)
PITCHER, Caroline
 Diamond.(D) 1988 (ip)
SPENCE, Alan
 Its Colours They are Fine.(E) 1987
 (ip)

CIVIL WAR

COLLISON-MORLEY, Kathleen
 Civil War at the Rectory.(E) 1980 (ip)
LEESON, Robert
 White Horse.(E) 1977 (ip)
MONTAGUE, Jeanne
 Lady Cavalier.(E) 1989 (op)
 Lady Cavalier Rides out.(E) 1989
 (op)

CLAIRVOYANCY

ROSE, Malcolm
 Rift.(E) 1985 (ip)

CLOTHES

BULL, Angela
 Green Gloves.(C) 1987 (ip)
 Pink Socks.(C) 1990 (ip)

CLUMSINESS

CARRICK, Malcolm
 Butterfingers.(B) 1985 (ip)
POWLING, Chris
 Butterfingers.(C) 1991 (ip)

COAL MINING

GATES, Susan P.
 Dragline.(D/E) 1991 (ip)
GRICE, Frederick
 Bonny Pit Laddie.(D/E) 1980 (ip)
KENWORTHY, John
 Running Riot.(D/E) 1990 (ip)
MOONEY, Bel
 Flower of Jet.(D/E) 1990 (ip)
PRICE, Susan
 Twopence a Tub.(E) 1991 (ip)

COLUMBUS

LAWSON, Robert
 I Discover Columbus.(D) 1992 (ip)

COMICS

LAIRD, Elizabeth
 Crackers.(D) 1990 (ip)

COMMUNICATIONS

KAYE, Geraldine
 Sky-blue Dragon.(C) 1983 (ip)
LAIRD, Elizabeth
 Crackers.(D) 1990 (ip)

COMPUTERS

ALLEN, Joy
 Computer for Charlie.(B) 1987 (ip)
BYARS, Betsy
 Computer Nut.(D/E) 1984 (ip)
CROSS, Gillian
 Demon Headmaster.(D) 1982 (ip)
 Prime Minister's Brain.(D) 1991 (ip)
DAVIES, Russell
 Dark Season.(E) 1991 (ip)
DICKS, Terrance
 Criminal Computer.(D) 1987 (op)
MACKAY, Claire
 Minerva Programme.(D) 1987 (ip)
NICHOLLS, Christopher
 Stolen Property.(D) 1990 (ip)
RUFFELL, Ann
 Computer Cheat.(C) 1987 (op)
SNELL, Gordon
 Tom's Amazing Machine.(D/E) 1988
 (ip)
 Tom's Amazing Machine Takes a
 Trip.(D/E) 1990 (ip)
 Tom's Amazing Machine Zaps
 Back.(D/E) 1989 (ip)
WATTS, Marilyn
 Graphicat.(D) 1991 (ip)

CONKERS

POWLING, Chris
 Conker as Hard as a Diamond.(C)
 1985 (ip)

CONSCIENTIOUS OBJECTORS

DARKE, Marjorie
 Long Way to Go.(E) 1989 (ip)

CONSERVATION AND POLLUTION

ALLEN, Judy
  Awaiting Developments.(C) 1989 (ip)
ASHTON, Jay
  Looking for Ilyriand.(E) 1990 (ip)
BRANFIELD, John
  Falklands Summer.(E) 1989 (op)
BURT, Roger
  Melanie Pluckrose Effect.(E) 1991 (ip)
COONTZ, Otto
  Night Walkers.(E) 1988 (ip)
CROSS, Gillian
  Rescuing Gloria.(C) 1989 (op)
DANN, Colin
  Animals of Farthing Wood.(D) 1979 (ip)
  In the Grip of Winter.(E) 1982 (ip)
  In the Path of the Storm.(D) 1991 (ip)
FISK, Nicholas
  Hole in the Head.(D/E) 1991 (ip)
HUNTER, Aileen
  Green Gang.(D) 1992 (ip)
JARMAN, Julia
  Ghost of Tantony Pig.(D) 1990 (ip)
KERVEN, Rosalind
  Mysteries of the Seals.(D) 1989 (ip)
  Sea is Singing.(D) 1987 (ip)
LIMB, Sue
  Trees Rule OK!(D) 1988 (ip)
MASTERS, Anthony
  Spirit of the Condor.(D) 1991 (ip)
MAYNE, William
  Farm That Ran out of Names.(D/E) 1990 (ip)
MCCAUGHREN, Tom
  Run to the Ark.(D/E) 1991 (ip)
MORPURGO, Michael
  Colly's Barn.(C) 1991 (ip)
  When the Whales Came.(D/E) 1985 (ip)
OWEN, Gareth
  Never Walk Alone.(D/E) 1991 (ip)
  Saving Grace.(D/E) 1989 (ip)
PEARSON, Maggie
  Save This Tree.(C) 1991 (ip)
PHIPSON, Joan
  Bird Smuggler.(D) 1977 (ip)
PILLING, Ann
  Dustbin Charlie.(C) 1988 (ip)

REES, David
  House That Moved.(C) 1982 (ip)
RENIER, Elizabeth
  Night of the Storm.(C) 1986 (ip)
ROWLANDS, Avril
  Poll.(D) 1991 (ip)
SADDLER, Allen
  Smudger's Seaside Spectacular.(D) 1986 (ip)
SMITH, Alexander McCall
  Akimbo and the Elephants.(C/D) 1990 (ip)
SMUCKER, Barbara Claassen
  Jacob's Little Giant.(D) 1987 (ip)
THOMPSON, Howard
  Battle of Billy's Pond.(D/E) 1977 (ip)
WALLACE, Karen
  Battle for Gold Diggers Forest.(B) 1990 (ip)
WARBURTON, Nick
  Battle of Baked Bean Alley.(D) 1992 (ip)
WATSON, James
  Where Nobody Sees.(E) 1987 (ip)
WHEATLEY, Nadia
  Blooding.(E) 1987 (ip)
WISEMAN, David
  Adam's Common.(E) 1989 (ip)

COOKING See FOOD AND COOKING

CORNWALL

BRANFIELD, John
  Fox in Winter.(E) 1980 (ip)

CORNWALL – MYTHS AND LEGENDS

QUAYLE, Eric
  Magic Ointment and Other Cornish Legends.(D) 1986 (ip)

COUNTRIES See INDIVIDUAL COUNTRIES

COUNTRY LIFE See also FARMS

ANDERSON, Rachel
  Poacher's Son.(D) 1986 (ip)

BARNETT, Gillian
  Gumboots and Other Risks.(D) 1990
  (ip)
BEACHCROFT, Nina
  Well Met by Witchlight.(C) 1990 (ip)
BELL, Eileen
  Tales from the End Cottage.(C/D)
  1970 (ip)
CHARD, Brigid
  Summer for a Lifetime.(D/E) 1975
  (ip)
CLEVELAND-PECK, Patricia
  Ark Angel.(C) 1991 (ip)
COCKETT, Mary
  Tracker.(C) 1984 (ip)

COWBOYS See AMERICAN WEST

COWS

FARRELL, Sally
  Rosina and Her Calf.(C) 1984 (op)

CRICKET

CHILDS, Rob
  Big Hit.(D) 1991 (ip)
  Sandford in to Bat.(D) 1985 (op)
DRAKE, Tony
  Half a Chance.(D/E) 1982 (ip)
  Playing it Right.(C/D) 1979 (ip)
HARDCASTLE, Michael
  Second Chance.(E) 1991 (ip)
TULLY, Tom
  Magnificent 11.(D) 1986 (ip)

CROCODILES

HACKNEY, Jo
  Alec's Dragon.(C) 1990 (ip)

CRUSADES

TREECE, Henry
  Children's Crusade.(D/E) 1970 (ip)

CUBS

ANDREWS, Stephen
  Cubs Series.(C) 1980 (ip)

CURVATURE OF THE SPINE

BLUME, Judy
  Deenie.(D/E) 1980 (ip)

CYCLE RACING

HACKLES, Lynn
  Racing Start.(D/E) 1991 (ip)

DAMS

MAYNE, William
  Farm That Ran out of Names.(D/E)
  1991 (ip)

DANCING See BALLET

DEAFNESS

DUNBAR, Joyce
  Mundo and the Weather-child.(D)
  1987 (ip)
FORWARD, Toby
  Toad Lady.(D) 1991 (ip)
HANLON, Emily
  Swing.(E) 1984 (ip)
URE, Jean
  Cool Simon.(D) 1990 (ip)
YEATMAN, Linda
  Dog Who Was More Than a
  Friend.(D) 1985 (ip)

DEATH

ALLEN, Judy
  Barriers.(E) 1981 (ip)
BAILLIE, Allan
  China Coin.(E) 1991 (ip)
BAUER, Marion Dane
  On My Honour.(D) 1989 (ip)
BLUME, Judy
  Tiger Eyes.(E) 1983 (ip)
BUNTING, Eve
  Sudden Silence.(E) 1991 (ip)
BYARS, Betsy
  Goodbye, Chicken Little.(E) 1982
  (ip)
DEAVER, Julie Reece
  Say Goodnight, Gracie.(E) 1988 ip
DILWORTH, Mary
  Island.(E) 1991 (ip)
FENTON, Edward
  Morning of the Gods.(E) 1987 (ip)
HAMLEY, Dennis
  Hare's Choice.(D) 1988 (ip)
HATHORN, Libby
  Thunderwith.(E) 1991 (op)

HELLBERG, Hans-Eric
Ben's Lucky Hat.(D) 1980 (ip)
IRWIN, Hadley
So Long at the Fair.(E) 1991 (ip)
LITTLE, Jean
Mama's Going to Buy You a Mock-
ingbird.(D/E) 1986 (ip)
LLOYD, Carole
Charlie Barber Treatment.(E) 1990
(ip)
LORENTZEN, Karen
Lanky Longlegs.(C/D) 1982 (ip)
MARINO, Jan
Eighty-eight Steps to
September.(D/E) 1990 (op)
SCOTT, Michael
Judith and the Traveller.(E) 1991 (ip)
SMITH, Doris Buchanan
Taste of Blackberries.(C/D) 1987 (ip)
WORRALL, Ann
Flash of Blue.(D/E) 1985 (ip)

DEBT

EHRLICH, Amy
Dark Card.(E) 1991 (ip)

DEER

FORTESCUE, J.W.
Story of a Red Deer.(D/E) 1985 (ip)

DENTISTS

ALLEN, Joy
Teeth for Charlie.(B) 1976 (ip)

DESIGN

FINE, Anne
Design a Pram.(C/D) 1991 (ip)
WATTS, Marilyn
Graphicat.(D) 1991 (ip)

DIABETES

TALBERT, Marc
Thin Ice.(E) 1989 (ip)

DINOSAURS

ARKLE, Phyllis
Dinosaur Field.(D) 1989 (ip)
Two Village Dinosaurs.(C) 1981 (ip)
Village Dinosaur.(C) 1979 (ip)

CORBETT, W.J.
Dear Grumble.(D) 1991 (ip)
HALL, Willis
Henry Hollins and the Dinosaur.(C)
1988 (ip)
LEROY, Margaret
Aristotle Sludge.(C) 1991 (ip)
PARISH, Peggy
Dinosaur Time.(B) 1974 (ip)
RICHLER, Mordecai
Jacob Two-two and the Dinosaur.(D)
1987 (ip)

DISABILITY See MENTALLY HANDICAPPED, PHYSICAL DISABILITY

DISASTERS

WESLEY, Mary
Sixth Seal.(E) 1984 (ip)

DISFIGUREMENT

HERLIHY, Dirlie
Ludie's Song.(D/E) 1990 (op)

DIVORCE

ADLER, C.S.
Binding Ties.(E) 1988 (op)
BLUME, Judy
It's Not the End of the World.(D/E)
1986 (ip)
CHARNEY, Sappho
Secret Family.(E) 1991 (ip)
DANZIGER, Paula
Divorce Express.(E) 1986 (ip)
FINE, Anne
Madame Doubtfire.(E) 1989 (ip)
JACOBS, Barbara
Stick.(D) 1988 (ip)
MURPHY, Jill
Worlds Apart.(C) 1988 (ip)
WILSON, Jacqueline
Suitcase Kid.(D) 1992 (ip)

DODOS

KING-SMITH, Dick
Dodos are Forever.(D) 1989 (ip)

DOGS See also GREYHOUND RACING

ARMSTRONG, William H.
  Sounder.(E) 1973 (ip)
ATKINSON, E.
  Greyfriars Bobby.(D/E) n.d. (ip)
BAKER, Ivy
  Monday Sheepdog.(E) 1987 (op)
BECKWITH, Lillian
  Spuddy.(E) 1988 (op)
BYTHEWAY, David
  Flash the Fire Dog.(D) 1984 (ip)
CALVERT, Patricia
  Hour of the Wolf.(D/E) 1983 (ip)
CATE, Dick
  Ghost Dog.(D/E) 1987 (ip)
  Old Dog, New Tricks.(C) 1980 (ip)
  Scared!(C) 1989 (ip)
CLARKE, Norma
  Patrick in Person.(D) 1991 (ip)
COOKSON, Catherine
  Bill and the "Mary Ann Shaughnes-
  sy".(D/E) 1991 (ip)
CUNLIFFE, John
  Our Sam: the Daftest Dog in the
  World.(D) 1980 (ip)
DANN, Colin
  Beach Dogs.(D) 1988 (ip)
  Just Nuffin.(D) 1989 (ip)
DE MESSIERES, Nicole
  Reina the Greyhound.(E) 1988 (ip)
DE ROO, Anne
  Traveller.(E) 1979 (ip)
DEJONG, Meindert
  Along Came a Dog.(D) 1971 (ip)
  Puppy Summer.(D) 1966 (ip)
DINAN, Carolyn
  Dog Would be Better.(B) 1987 (ip)
EARNSHAW, Brian
  Rock Dog Gang.(D) 1987 (ip)
ESTES, Eleanor
  Ginger Pye.(D) 1951 (ip)
FIDLER, Kathleen
  Flash the Sheepdog.(D) 1984 (ip)
  Turk the Border Collie.(D) 1986 (ip)
FURMINGER, Justine
  Hopeless Harry.(C) 1990 (ip)
GRANT, Gwen
  Gypsy Racer.(D) 1991 (ip)
GRIFFITH, Helen V.
  Foxy.(D) 1990 (ip)

GRIFFITHS, Helen
  Just dog.(D) 1974 (ip)
HATHORN, Libby
  Thunderwith.(E) 1991 (op)
IMPEY, Rose
  Houdini Dog.(C) 1988 (ip)
KING-SMITH, Dick
  Dumpling.(B) 1986 (ip)
  Lightning Strikes Twice.(C) 1991 (ip)
  Yob.(C) 1986 (ip)
LAVELLE, Sheila
  Fetch the Slipper.(B) 1989 (ip)
  Harry's Dog.(B) 1988 (ip)
LITTLE, Jean
  Lost and Found.(C) 1987 (ip)
LONDON, Jack
  Call of the Wild.(E) 1992 (ip)
  White Fang.(E) 1991 (ip)
MORPURGO, Michael
  Conker.(C) 1987 (ip)
NAUGHTON, Bill
  Dog Called Nelson.(D) 1978 (ip)
OLDFIELD, Pamela
  Shaggy Dog Story.(C) 1990 (ip)
PEARCE, Philippa
  Dog So Small.(D/E) 1970 (ip)
POWLING, Chris
  Hoppity-gap.(C) 1988 (ip)
PULLEIN-THOMPSON, Christine
  Careless Ben.(B) 1988 (op)
SMITH, Roger
  Olly.(C/D) 1989 (ip)
STRONG, Jeremy
  Dogs are Different.(C) 1987 (ip)
WEST, Colin
  Monty Bites Back.(C) 1990 (ip)
  Monty, the Dog Who Wears
  Glasses.(C) 1989 (ip)
WHYBROW, Ian
  Sniff and the Secret of Spalderton
  Hall.(D) 1991 (ip)
  Sniff Bounces Back.(D) 1991 (ip)
  Sniff Stories.(D) 1989 (ip)
WILLSON, Robina Beckles
  Square Bear.(C) 1983 (ip)
WILSON, David Henry
  Superdog.(C) 1987 (op)
  Superdog in Trouble.(C) 1988 (op)
  Superdog the Hero.(C) 1987 (op)
WILSON, Jacqueline
  Werepuppy.(C) 1991 (ip)

DOLLS See TOYS AND DOLLS

DOLPHINS

KENDALL, Sarita
 Ransom for a River Dolphin.(C) 1992 (ip)

DONKEYS

COCKETT, Mary
 School Donkey.(C) 1982 (ip)
HUGHSON, Anne
 Donkey Days.(B/C) 1991 (ip)
KAYE, Geraldine
 Donkey Christmas.(C) 1988 (ip)
 Donkey Strike.(C) 1984 (op)
 Plum Tree Party.(C) 1982 (op)
LAMPLUGH, Lois
 Winter Donkey.(D) 1980 (ip)
OLDFIELD, Pamela
 Toby and the Donkey.(C) 1986 (ip)
PINTO, Jacqueline
 School Donkey Disaster.(C) 1988 (op)

DOWN'S SYNDROME

ANDERSON, Rachel
 Best Friends.(C) 1991 (ip)
 Jessy Runs Away.(C) 1988 (ip)
HERSOM, Kathleen
 Half-child.(D/E) 1989 (ip)

DRAGONS

ASHTON, Charles
 Jet Smoke and Dragon Fire.(E) 1991 (ip)
ASHTON, Jay
 Looking for Ilyriand.(E) 1992 (ip)
BATTEN, Ralph
 Kingdom of the Carpet Dragon.(D) 1989 (ip)
CASS, Joan
 Book of Dragons.(D) 1988 (op)
 Dragon Who Grew.(C) 1987 (op)
CAVE, Kathryn
 Dragonrise.(C) 1988 (op)
COUNSEL, June
 Dragon in Class 4.(C) 1991 (ip)
 Dragon in Spring Term.(C) 1988 (ip)
 Dragon in Summer.(C) 1990 (ip)
CRESSWELL, Helen
 Dragon Ride.(C) 1987 (ip)

CUNLIFFE, John
 Great Dragon Competition and Other Stories.(D) 1973 (ip)
FLEETWOOD, Jenni
 Ice-cream Dragon.(C) 1990 (ip)
GRAHAME, Kenneth
 Reluctant Dragon.(C) 1983 (ip)
GREAVES, Margaret
 Charlie, Emma and the Runaway Dragon.(C) 1991 (op)
HOLIDAY, Jane
 Floella Hits the Roof.(C) 1989 (ip)
JOY, Margaret
 Gran's Dragons.(D) 1980 (ip)
JUNGMAN, Ann
 Little Dragon Steps Out.(C) 1989 (ip)
LIVELY, Penelope
 Dragon Trouble.(C) 1984 (ip)
MANNING, Rosemary
 Dragon in Danger.(D) 1971 (ip)
 Dragon in the Harbour.(D) 1982 (ip)
 Dragon's Quest.(D) 1974 (ip)
 Green Smoke.(D) 1967 (ip)
MANNING-SANDERS, Ruth
 Book of Dragons.(D) 1964 (ip)
POWLING, Chris
 Bella's Dragon.(C) 1988 (ip)
PRINCE, Maggie
 Dragon in the Drainpipe.(C) 1981 (op)
 Dragon in the Family.(C) 1985 (op)
RUFFELL, Ann
 Dragon Air.(C) 1989 (ip)
 Dragon Earth.(C) 1981 (ip)
 Dragon Wanted.(C) 1986 (op)
 Dragon Water.(C) 1989 (ip)
SIMISTER, Jean
 Where Dragons Breathe.(D) 1986 (ip)
SLEIGH, Barbara
 Ninety-nine Dragons.(D) 1977 (ip)
SPEIGHT, Margot
 Murdo.(D) 1983 (ip)
UMANSKY, Kaye
 Big Iggy.(D) 1987 (ip)
VACHER, Gwyneth
 Dragon and the Magic Stone.(C) 1986 (op)
WHITEHEAD, Andrew
 Desperate Dragons.(C) 1991 (ip)
YOLEN, Jane
 Dragon's Blood.(D/E) 1982 (ip)

DROUGHT

HO, Minfong
Rice without Rain.(E) 1986 (ip)
O'NEILL, Judith
Deepwater.(D/E) 1989 (op)

DRUG ADDICTION

CHILDRESS, Alice
Hero Ain't Nothing But a
Sandwich.(E) 1973 (ip)
CONRAD, Pam
Taking the Ferry Home.(E) 1990 (ip)

DRUIDS

MACKEN, Walter
Island of the Great Yellow Ox.(D/E)
1972 (ip)
MELLING, O. R.
Druid's Tune.(E) 1992 (ip)
Singing Stone.(E) 1986 (ip)

DRUMS

OWEN, Gareth
Douglas the Drummer.(C) 1991 (ip)

DUCKS

LAWHEAD, Stephen
Tale of Timothy Mallard.(C) 1990 (ip)
MATTINGLEY, Christobel
Duck Boy.(C) 1983 (ip)
MORGAN, Alison
Bright-eye.(C) 1985 (ip)

DWARVES See FAIRY PEOPLE

DYSLEXIA

KENNEMORE, Tim
Wall of Words.(D/E) 1984 (op)

EAGLES

MAYNE, William
Antar and the Eagles.(D) 1989 (ip)
McBRATNEY, Sam
Claudius Bald Eagle.(D) 1987 (ip)

EARTHQUAKES

DUNLOP, Bevereley
Earthquake Town.(D/E) 1985 (ip)

HARDCASTLE, Michael
Quake.(D) 1988 (ip)
SALKEY, Andrew
Earthquake.(E) 1971 (ip)

EAST ANGLIA

HAYES, Rosemary
Flight of the Mallard.(D) 1989 (ip)

EAST ANGLIA – FOLK TALES

CROSSLEY-HOLLAND, Kevin
Dead Moon and Other Tales from
East Anglia and the Fen Country.(E)
1990 (ip)
PEARSON, Maggie
Strong Tom.(C) 1988 (ip)

EAST BERLIN

LUTZEIER, Elizabeth
Wall.(E) 1991 (ip)

EASTER

RUFFELL, Ann
Grand Bristleton Easter Egg.(C) 1988
(ip)

EDWARDIAN PERIOD

ALLAN, Mabel Esther
Mills down below.(E) 1980 (op)
ANDERSON, Rachel
Poacher's Son.(D) 1986 (ip)
APPS, Roy
Secret Summer of Daniel Lyons.(E)
1991 (ip)
AVERY, Gillian
Likely Lad.(E) 1992 (ip)
BAWDEN, Nina
Peppermint Pig.(E) 1977 (ip)
BURNETT, Frances Hodgson
Secret Garden.(E) 1992 (ip)
COLLINSON, Roger
Paper Flags and Penny Ices.(D) 1984
(ip)
FAIRFAX-LUCY, Brian
Children of Charlecote.(D/E) 1989
(ip)
NESBIT, E.
Railway Children.(D/E) 1991 (ip)
WILLS, Jean
Lily and Lorna.(C) 1991 (ip)

19

EGYPT See also ANCIENT EGYPT

SAMPSON, Derek A.
Follow That Pharoah.(D) 1989 (ip)

EIGHTEENTH CENTURY See also APPRENTICES

DARKE, Marjorie
First of Midnight.(E) 1989 (ip)
GARFIELD, Leon
Devil in the Fog.(D/E) 1970 (ip)
Jack Holborn.(E) 1970 (ip)
HUNTER, Mollie
Lothian Run.(E) 1984 (ip)
KAVANAGH, P.J.
Scarf Jack.(E) 1980 (ip)
MCGREGOR, Iona
Edinburgh Reel.(E) 1986 (ip)
WELCH, Ronald
Captain of Dragoons.(E) 1974 (ip)

ELECTIVE MUTE

ASHLEY, Bernard
Trouble with Donovan Croft.(D/E)
1977 (ip)
BECKWITH, Lillian
Spuddy.(E) 1988 (ip)
STORR, Catherine
Boy and the Swan.(D) 1987 (ip)

ELEMENTS

HESLEWOOD, Juliet
Earth, Air, Fire and Water.(D) 1985
(ip)

ELEPHANTS

MATTHEWS, Andrew
Loads of Trouble.(D) 1991 (op)
SLOAN, Carolyn
Elephant for Muthu.(D) 1986 (ip)

ELIZABETIIAN PERIOD

ALLEN, Gillian
Twins of the Black Bear Inn.(C/D)
1991 (ip)
MORPURGO, Michael
My Friend Walter.(D) 1988 (ip)
TREASE, Geoffrey
Cue for Treason.(D/E) 1970 (ip)

ELVES See FAIRY PEOPLE

EMIGRATION

ALINGTON, Gabriel
Stars are Upside Down.(D/E) 1991
(ip)
DILLON, Eilis
Seekers.(E) 1991 (ip)

ENGLAND – FOLK TALES

CROSSLEY-HOLLAND, Kevin
British and Irish Folk Tales.(C/D)
1990 (ip)
GARNER, Alan
Bag of Moonshine.(D/E) 1986 (ip)
JACOBS, Joseph
English Fairy Tales.(C/D) 1980 (ip)

EPILEPSY

YOUNG, Helen
What Difference Does it Make,
Danny?(C/D) 1980 (ip)

EQUAL OPPORTUNITIES

KAYE, Geraldine
Snow Girl.(C) 1991 (ip)

ESKIMO See INUIT

EVACUATION

BAWDEN, Nina
Carrie's War.(D) 1973 (ip)
Keeping Henry.(D) 1988 (ip)
LIVELY, Penelope
Going Back.(E) 1975 (ip)
MAGORIAN, Michelle
Back Home.(E) 1985 (ip)
Goodnight Mr. Tom.(E) 1983 (ip)
STREATFEILD, Noel
Curtain Up.(D/E) 1983 (ip)

EYAM

DOHERTY, Berlie
Children of Winter.(D/E) 1985 (ip)
WALSH, Jill Paton
Parcel of Patterns.(D/E) 1989 (ip)

FABLES

AESOP
Fables.(D) 1992 (ip)
COHEN, Mark
Puffin Book of Fabulous Fables.(C) 1991 (ip)

FAIRS

BEDFORD, William
Golden Gallopers.(C) 1991 (ip)
SILVESTRE, Ruth
Old Woman Who Lived in a Round-about.(C) 1991 (ip)

FAIRY PEOPLE

AIKEN, Joan
Kitchen Warriors.(C/D) 1983 (ip)
BANKS, Lynne Reid
Fairy Rebel.(D) 1987 (ip)
BENNETT, Leonie
Kat's Goblin.(D) 1990 (ip)
BIEGEL, Paul
Dwarfs of Nosegay.(D) 1980 (ip)
Virgil Nosegay and the Cake-hunt.(D) 1981 (op)
Virgil Nosegay and the Hupmobile.(D) 1983 (op)
CURLEY, Chris
Doorkeepers.(D) 1989 (ip)
HILL, Douglas
Goblin Party.(C) 1988 (ip)
KING-SMITH, Dick
Paddy's Pot of Gold.(D) 1990 (ip)
PEARSON, Maggie
Peter Pepper and the Goblin.(C) 1989 (ip)

FAIRY TALES

AIKEN, Joan
Last Slice of Rainbow and Other Stories.(C/D) 1985 (ip)
Tale of a One-way Street.(D) 1978 (ip)
JACOBS, Joseph
Celtic Fairy Tales.(D/E) 1968 (ip)
English Fairy Tales.(C/D) 1968 (ip)
JONES, Terry
Fairy Tales.(C/D) 1981 (ip)
PHILLIP, Neil
Fairy Tales of Eastern Europe.(C/D) 1992 (ip)

PIERCE, Patricia
Country Life Book of Fairy Tales.(D) 1985 (ip)

FALCONS

CANNING, Victor
Painted Tent.(E) 1979 (ip)

FALKLANDS WAR

BRANFIELD, John
Falklands Summer.(E) 1989 (op)
MARK, Jan
Hillingdon Fox.(E) 1991 (ip)
MILLER, Moira
Did You Think I Would Leave You Crying?(D/E) 1991 (ip)

FAMILIES

BAWDEN, Nina
Outside Child.(E) 1992 (ip)
BYARS, Betsy
Blossom Promise.(C/D) 1989 (ip)
Blossoms and the Green Phantom.(C/D) 1988 (ip)
Blossoms Meet the Vulture Lady.(C/D) 1988 (ip)
DESAI, Anita
Village by the Sea.(E) 1992 (ip)
HARRISON, Maggie
Angels on Roller Skates.(B) 1990 (ip)
HOWARD, Ellen
Sister.(E) 1992 (ip)
HUGHSON, Anne
Rag Bag.(B/C) 1984 (ip)
KING-SMITH, Dick
Friends and Brothers.(C) 1987 (ip)
LAMBERT, Thelma
Benny the Boaster.(B) 1988 (ip)
LIVELY, Penelope
Driftway.(D/E) 1972 (ip)
MILLER, Moira
What Size is Andy?(C) 1984 (ip)
NIMMO, Jenny
Tatty Apple.(D) 1984 (ip)
NOSTLINGER, Christine
But Jasper Came Instead.(E) 1986 (op)
PARK, Ruth
Callie's Family.(D) 1988 (ip)
PEARCE, Philippa
Way to Sattin Shore.(D/E) 1985 (ip)

THOMPSON, Pat
  Family Gathering.(D) 1987 (ip)

FAMILY HISTORY

BULL, Angela
  Up the Attic Stairs.(E) 1989 (ip)

FAMILY RELATIONSHIPS See also SPECIFIC FAMILY RELATIONSHIPS and RELATIONSHIPS

ALCOCK, Vivien
  Cuckoo Sister.(D/E) 1985 (ip)
ASHLEY, Bernard
  Seeing Off Uncle Jack.(E) 1991 (ip)
BRADMAN, Tony
  Love Them, Hate Them.(D) 1991 (ip)
  You're Late, Dad.(E) 1991 (ip)
BURNS, Peggy
  Splitting Image of Rosie Brown.(E) 1989 (ip)
BYARS, Betsy
  Animal, the Vegetable and John D Jones.(E) 1984 (ip)
  Bingo Brown and the Language of Love.(E) 1990 (ip)
  Bingo Brown, Gipsy Lover.(E) 1991 (ip)
  Two Thousand Pound Goldfish.(D) 1984 (ip)
COLLURA, Mary-Ellen Lang
  Jordy.(D/E) 1988 (ip)
CORLETT, William
  Bloxworth Blue.(E) 1984 (op)
CROSS, Gillian
  Roscoe's Leap.(E) 1987 (ip)
DARKE, Jo
  Josie and Grandpa.(C) 1987 (ip)
FINE, Anne
  Book of the Banshee.(E) 1991 (ip)
  Crummy Mummy and Me.(D) 1988 (ip)
  Madame Doubtfire.(E) 1990 (ip)
  Round Behind the Ice-house.(E) 1990 (ip)
FISK, Pauline
  Midnight Blue.(E) 1990 (ip)
HOWKER, Janni
  Isaac Campion.(D/E) 1987 (ip)
NOSTLINGER, Christine
  Marrying Off Mother.(D) 1986 (op)

PATERSON, Katherine
  Park's Quest.(D/E) 1989 (ip)
POPLE, Maureen
  Other Side of the Family.(E) 1989 (ip)
PULLMAN, Philip
  Broken Bridge.(D/E) 1990 (ip)
STORR, Catherine
  Boy and the Swan.(D) 1987 (ip)
STREATFEILD, Noel
  Vicarage Family.(D/E) 1977 (ip)
ZABEL, Jennifer
  Under the Pudding Basin.(C) 1989 (ip)

FAMINE

CONLAN-MCKENNA, M.
  Under the Hawthorn Tree.(D/E) 1990 (ip)
LUTZEIER, Elizabeth
  Coldest Winter.(E) 1991 (ip)

FARMING See also CITY FARMS and SHEEP AND SHEEP-FARMING

GARDAM, Jane
  Bridget and William.(C) 1981 (ip)
  Kit.(C) 1983 (ip)
GOWANS, Elizabeth
  Shepherd's Flock.(D) 1986 (op)
O'NEILL, Judith
  Stringybark Summer.(D/E) 1990 (ip)
WHITE, E. B.
  Charlotte's Web.(D) 1969 (ip)
WILLARD, Barbara
  Farmer's Boy.(D) 1991 (ip)
WILLIAMS, Susan
  Lambing at Sheepfold Farm.(C/D) 1982 (ip)
  Winter Comes to Sheepfold Farm.(C/D) 1984 (ip)

FEARS AND PHOBIAS

DALGLIESH, Alice
  Bears of Hemlock Mountain.(C) 1973 (ip)
HILL, Susan
  One Night at a Time.(C) 1984 (ip)
LITTLE, Jean
  Different Dragons.(C/D) 1988 (ip)
MARK, Jan
  Nothing to be Afraid of.(D/E) 1982 (ip)

TOMLINSON, Jill
Owl Who was Afraid of the
Dark.(B/C) 1968 (ip)

FEMINISM

ADLER, Susan
Mightier than the Lipstick.(E) 1990
(ip)
CORBALIS, Judy
Wrestling Princess and Other
Stories.(C/D) 1986 (ip)

FEN COUNTRY See EAST ANGLIA

FESTIVALS See also INDIVIDUAL FESTIVALS

SAMPSON, Fay
Chris and the Dragon.(C) 1985 (ip)

FETES

ROMANES, Alexa
Red Letter Day.(C) 1986 (ip)

FEUDS

MAYNE, William
Ravensgill.(D/E) 1990 (ip)
While the Bells Ring.(D) 1979 (ip)
SUTCLIFF, Rosemary
Blood Feud.(E) 1978 (ip)

FIFTEENTH CENTURY

DEARY, Terry
Witch in Time.(C) 1987 (ip)
HARNETT, Cynthia
Wool-pack.(E) n.d. (ip)
Writing on the Hearth.(E) 1971 (ip)
WILLARD, Barbara
Miller's Boy.(D/E) 1976 (ip)

FIFTH CENTURY

KING, Clive
Ninny's Boat.(D/E) 1980 (ip)

FILMS

APPS, Roy
Secret Summer of Daniel Lyons.(E)
1991 (ip)
BILLINGTON, Rachel
Star Time.(E) 1984 (ip)

SMITH, Alexander McCall
Film Boy.(C) 1989 (ip)
STREATFEILD, Noel
Painted Garden.(D/E) 1969 (ip)

FIRE

BOND, Ruskin
Flames in the Forest.(C/D) 1988 (ip)
CARR, Roger Vaughan
Firestorm!(E) 1985 (ip)
SOUTHALL, Ivan
Ash Road.(D/E) 1972 (ip)

FLEAS See PERFORMING FLEAS

FLIGHT

SCOTT, Tim
Colin and the Paper Dart.(C) 1991
(ip)
SEFTON, Catherine
Flying Sam.(B) 1986 (ip)

FLOODS

BAILLIE, Allan
Hero.(D/E) 1991 (ip)
BRINSMEAD, Hesba Fay
When You Come to the Ferry.(D)
1988 (op)
WADDELL, Martin
Little Obie and the Flood.(C) 1991
(ip)

FOLK TALES See also INDIVIDUAL COUNTRIES and AREAS

AIKEN, Joan
Fog Hounds, Wind Cat, Sea
Mice.(C/D) 1987 (op)
Kingdom Under the Sea.(C) 1971 (ip)
BRYAN, Ashley
Beat the Story-drum, Pum-
Pum.(C/D) 1980 (ip)
HAYES, Barbara
Folk Tales and Fables of the
World.(C/D/E) 1987 (ip)
LURIE, Alison
Clever Gretchen and Other Forgotten
Folk Tales.(D) 1991 (ip)
WILLIAMS-ELLIS, Amabel
Enchanted World.(D) 1988 (ip)

23

FOOD AND COOKING

CRESSWELL, Helen
  Piemakers.(C/D) 1976 (ip)
DAHL, Roald
  Charlie and the Chocolate
  Factory.(C/D) 1991 (ip)
HUNT, Peter
  Sue and the Honey Machine.(C) 1989
  (ip)
LORD, John Vernon
  Giant Jam Sandwich.(C) 1972 (ip)
MAISNER, Heather
  Yummy Yuk.(C) 1990 (ip)
MATTHEWS, Andrew
  Dr Monsoon Taggert's Amazing Fin-
  ishing Academy.(D) 1990 (ip)
  Wolf Pie.(C) 1988 (op)
McBRATNEY, Sam
  Zesty Goes Cooking.(C) 1989 (op)
MITCHELL, Pratima
  Dadijan's Carrot Halvah.(C) 1988
  (ip)
OVERTON, Jenny
  Ship from Simnel Street.(D/E) 1986
  (ip)
PILLING, Ann
  Big Biscuit.(B) 1989 (ip)
RYAN, Margaret
  King Tubbitum and the Little
  Cook.(C) 1988 (ip)
SMITH, Alexander McCall
  Marzipan Max.(C) 1991 (ip)
  Perfect Hamburger.(C) 1984 (ip)
  Spaghetti Tangle.(C/D) 1992 (ip)
SMITH, Robert Kimmel
  Chocolate Fever.(C) 1989 (ip)
ZABEL, Jennifer
  Mr Berry's Ice Cream Parlour.(C)
  1984 (ip)

FOOTBALL

ALLEN, Joy
  County Rovers for Charlie.(B) 1988
  (ip)
  Cup Final for Charlie.(B) 1985 (ip)
  Goal for Charlie.(B) 1984 (ip)
BRADMAN, Tony
  One Nil.(C) 1987 (ip)
BREINBURG, Petronella
  Brinsly's Dream.(D) 1980 (ip)

BROWNE, Eileen
  Caraway and the Cup Final.(B) 1990
  (ip)
CHILDS, Rob
  Big Kick.(D) 1991 (ip)
  Big Match.(D) 1987 (ip)
  Sandford on Tour.(D) 1983 (ip)
HAMLEY, Dennis
  Dangleboots.(D) 1987 (ip)
HARDCASTLE, Michael
  Kick Off.(E) 1986 (ip)
  Mascot.(D) 1991 (ip)
  Penalty.(E) 1990 (ip)
  Second Chance.(E) 1991 (ip)
  Team That Wouldn't Give in.(D)
  1990 (ip)
JOY, Margaret
  See You at the Match.(C) 1987 (ip)
MCCANN, Sean
  Hot Shot!(E) 1981 (op)
  Shoot on Sight.(E) 1981 (op)
  Shooting Stars.(E) 1980 (op)
  Team That Nobody Wanted.(E) 1982
  (op)
TULLY, Tom
  Robbo Versus the World.(D) 1990
  (ip)
  Robbo 2.(D) 1990 (ip)
WADDELL, Martin
  Napper Goes for Goal.(D) 1981 (ip)
  Napper's Golden Goals.(D) 1984 (ip)
WADDELL, Sid
  Jossy's Giants.(D) 1986 (op)
WARBURTON, Nick
  Saving Grace.(C/D) 1989 (ip)

FOSSILS

CONRAD, Pam
  My Daniel.(E) 1991 (ip)
MAY, Kara
  Lenny's Dinosaur Bone.(C) 1990 (ip)

FOSTERING See ADOPTION AND FOSTERING

FOURTEENTH CENTURY

ATTERTON, Julian
  Tournament of Fortune.(E) 1985 (ip)

FOXES

BYARS, Betsy
  Midnight Fox.(D) 1976 (ip)
BYERS, Irene
  Fox on the Pavement.(D) 1984 (op)
DAHL, Roald
  Fantastic Mr Fox.(C/D) 1991 (ip)
DILLON, Eilis
  Family of Foxes.(D) 1992 (ip)
DUNLOP, Eileen
  Fox Farm.(D/E) 1987 (ip)
GRANT, Gwen
  Fox Fire.(C) 1991 (ip)
KAYE, Geraldine
  Sky-blue Dragon.(C) 1983 (ip)
KERVEN, Rosalind
  Who Ever Heard of a Vegetarian
  Fox?(D) 1990 (ip)
KILNER, Geoffey
  Prince of the Dustbins.(C/D) 1986 (ip)
KING-SMITH, Dick
  Fox Busters.(C/D) 1978 (ip)
LINDSAY, Gillian
  Fox Barn.(C) 1982 (ip)
MANNING-SANDERS, Ruth
  Fox Tales.(C) 1976 (ip)
MARSHALL, Edward
  Fox at Work.(B) 1991 (ip)
  Fox be Nimble.(B) 1991 (ip)
MCCAUGHREN, Tom
  Run Swift, Run Free.(D/E) 1986 (ip)
  Run to Earth.(D/E) 1985 (ip)
  Run with the Wind.(D/E) 1983 (ip)
MORPURGO, Michael
  Little Foxes.(D) 1990 (ip)
MORSE, Brian
  Sauce for the Fox.(D) 1989 (ip)
NIMMO, Jenny
  Red Secret.(C) 1989 (ip)
STRONG, Jeremy
  Fox on the Roof.(D) 1984 (ip)
THOMSON, David
  Danny Fox.(D) 1971 (ip)
  Danny Fox at the Palace.(D) 1976 (ip)
  Danny Fox Meets a Stranger.(D) 1968
  (ip)

FRANCE – MYTHS AND LEGENDS

PICARD, Barbara Leonie
  French Legends, Tales and Fairy
  Stories.(D) 1992 (ip)

FRENCH REVOLUTION

GARFIELD, Leon
  Revolution!(E) 1989 (ip)

FRIENDSHIP

ANDERSON, Rachel
  Best Friends.(C) 1991 (ip)
ASHER, Sandy
  Friends and Sisters.(E) 1983 (op)
BAWDEN, Nina
  Robbers.(E) 1979 (ip)
  Witch's Daughter.(D) 1966 (ip)
BLUME, Judy
  Iggie's House.(D) 1981 (ip)
  Just as Long as We're Together.(E)
  1987 (ip)
CORLETT, William
  Gate of Eden.(E) 1982 (op)
CREBBIN, June
  Best Friends.(C) 1990 (ip)
DICKINSON, Mary
  Alex and Roy – Best Friends.(C) 1988
  (ip)
FARISH, Terry
  Why I'm Already Blue.(E) 1992 (ip)
GREENE, Constance
  Girl Called AL.(D) 1969 (ip)
GUY, Rosa
  Friends.(E) 1974 (ip)
HOY, Linda
  Your Friend, Rebecca.(D/E) 1983
  (ip)
JACOBS, Barbara
  Stick.(D) 1990 (ip)
KLEIN, Robin
  Enemies.(D) 1985 (ip)
KORALEK, Jenny
  Going Out with Hatty.(D) 1989 (ip)
LAVELLE, Sheila
  My Best Fiend.(D) 1980 (ip)
LEESON, Robert
  Harold and Bella, Jammy and Me .(C)
  1980 (ip)
MACGIBBON, Jean
  Hal.(E) 1980 (ip)
MARK, Jan
  Dead Letter Box.(C) 1982 (ip)
  Thunder and Lightnings.(D/E) 1987
  (op)
ORGEL, Doris
  Devil in Vienna.(E) 1989 (ip)

PILLING, Ann
  On the Lion's Side.(D/E) 1988 (ip)
RICHEMONT, Enid
  Glass Bird.(D) 1990 (ip)
SACHS, Marilyn
  Secret Friend.(D) 1978 (ip)
URE, Jean
  Bottled Cherry Angel.(D/E) 1987 (ip)
  You Two.(E) 1985 (op)
WOODSON, Jacqueline
  Last Summer with Maizon.(D) 1992
  (ip)

FROGS

LEESON, Robert
  Never Kiss Frogs.(C) 1988 (ip)
  One Frog Too Many.(C) 1991 (ip)
LOBEL, Arnold
  Days with Frog and Toad.(B) 1992
  (ip)
  Frog and Toad All Year.(B) 1992 (ip)
  Frog and Toad are Friends.(B) 1992
  (ip)
  Frog and Toad Together.(B) 1992 (ip)
MASTERS, Anthony
  Frog.(D) 1990 (ip)
MUIR, Helen
  Lila the Edible Frog.(D) 1986 (ip)
SZUDEK, Agnes S.P.
  I've Got Frogs.(C) 1988 (op)
UMANSKY, Kaye
  Fwog Pwince: The Twuth!(C) 1989
  (ip)

FURNITURE

JONES, Diana Wynne
  Chair Person.(C) 1989 (ip)

GAMBLING

EHRLICH, Amy
  Dark Card.(E) 1991 (ip)

GANGS

ALLEN, Joy
  Adventure for Charlie.(B) 1986 (ip)
COLLINSON, Roger
  Get Lavinia Goodbody!(D) 1983 (ip)
JOY, Margaret
  Gertie's Gang.(C) 1990 (ip)
KAYE, Geraldine
  School Pool Gang.(C) 1989 (ip)

OLDFIELD, Pamela
  Gumby Gang Again.(C) 1986 (op)
  Gumby Gang Strikes Again.(C) 1984
  (op)
  More About the Gumby Gang.(C)
  1982 (op)
  Return of the Gumby Gang.(C) 1986
  (ip)
PEARCE, Philippa
  Elm Street Lot.(C) 1979 (ip)
QUIRK, Yvonne Coppard
  Copper's Kid.(D) 1989 (ip)
SEFTON, Catherine
  Finn Gang.(C) 1981 (ip)
  My Gang.(C) 1984 (ip)
SNELL, Gordon
  Red Spectacle's Gang.(D) 1991 (ip)

GARDENS AND GARDENING

BURNETT, Frances Hodgson
  Secret Garden.(D) 1975 (ip)
MANGEN, Anne
  Umbrella Tree.(B) 1989 (ip)
McCULLOCH, Christian
  Mr Potter's Gardening Magic.(C)
  1991 (ip)
PEARCE, Philippa
  Tom's Midnight Garden.(D) 1958 (ip)
SLOAN, Carolyn
  Skewer's Garden.(D) 1983 (ip)

GEESE

MANNING-SANDERS, Ruth
  Young Gabby Goose.(C) 1975 (ip)

GENETIC ENGINEERING

ALCOCK, Vivien
  Monster Garden.(D) 1992 (ip)

GENIES

BEACHCROFT, Nina
  Genie and Her Bottle.(D) 1992 (ip)
FINE, Anne
  Sudden Glow of Gold.(D) 1991 (ip)
  Sudden Puff of Glittering Smoke.(D)
  1989 (ip)
  Sudden Swirl of Icy Wind.(D) 1990
  (ip)
GEBLER, Carlo
  Television Genie.(C) 1989 (ip)

LEESON, Robert
  Genie on the Loose.(D/E) 1984 (ip)
  Third Class Genie.(D) 1975 (ip)
MORSE, Brian
  Nick and the Genie.(C) 1987 (ip)
SEFTON, Catherine
  Puff of Smoke.(C) 1988 (ip)

GEORGIAN PERIOD See also APPRENTICES

PEYTON, Kathleen M.
  Right-hand Man.(E) 1983 (op)

GERBILS

APPS, Roy
  Philomena Hall and the Best Kept Gerbil Competition.(C) 1991 (ip)
BRADMAN, Tony
  Gerbil Crazy.(B) 1990 (ip)
PEARCE, Philippa
  Battle of Bubble and Squeak.(C) 1978 (ip)

GERMANY – FOLK TALES

ROSEN, Michael
  Wicked Tricks of Till Owlyglass.(C/D) 1989 (ip)

GIANTS

CUNLIFFE, John
  Giant Kippernose and Other Stories.(C) 1972 (ip)
DAHL, Roald
  BFG.(C/D) 1991 (ip)
LEESON, Robert
  Reversible Giant.(C) 1988 (ip)
MANNING-SANDERS, Ruth
  Book of Giants.(D) 1982 (op)
PIROTTA, Saviour
  Giant Stepped on Joey's Toe.(B) 1990 (ip)
SLEIGH, Barbara
  Grimblegraw and the Wuthering Witch.(C) 1980 (op)
STEWART, Paul
  Giant Gutso and the Wacky Gang.(C) 1991 (ip)
STINTON, Judith
  Hurley Giants.(B) 1991 (ip)

WADDELL, Martin
  Class Three and the Beanstalk.(C) 1988 (ip)

GIFTED CHILDREN

DAHL, Roald
  Matilda.(C/D) 1992 (ip)

GINGERBREAD MEN

WALKER, Elizabeth
  Adventures of the Gingerbread Man.(C/D) 1989 (op)
  Gingerbread Man in Winter.(C/D) 1988 (op)

GLUE SNIFFING

AITKEN, Tom
  Water Lane.(E) 1986 (op)

GNOMES See FAIRY PEOPLE

GOATS

CROSS, Gillian
  Rescuing Gloria.(D) 1989 (op)
RUFFELL, Ann
  Goatbuster.(D) 1991 (op)

GOBLINS See FAIRY PEOPLE

GOLD

SEED, Jenny
  Gold Dust.(C) 1982 (ip)
THOMPSON, Valerie
  Gold on the Wind.(D/E) 1977 (ip)

GOLD PROSPECTING

ROCK, Nora
  Rope around the World.(D) 1980 (ip)

GORILLAS

BOSTON, Lucy M.
  Stranger at Green Knowe.(D/E) 1977 (ip)
TOMLINSON, Jill
  Gorilla Who Wanted to Grow Up.(C) 1991 (ip)

GRANDPARENTS

BRINSMEAD, Hesba Fay
  Pastures of the Blue Crane.(E) 1978 (ip)
BYARS, Betsy
  House of Wings.(D) 1977 (ip)
HARRISON, Maggie
  Lizzie's List.(D) 1991 (ip)
ROSSELSON, Leon
  Rosa's Grandfather Sings Again.(C) 1991 (ip)
  Rosa's Singing Grandfather.(C) 1991 (ip)
SHARPE, Hilary
  Adelaide's Naughty Granny.(C) 1990 (op)
SMITH, Robert Kimmel
  War with Grandpa.(D) 1989 (ip)
SUDBERY, Rodie
  Grandmother's Footsteps.(C) 1984 (ip)
THOMSON, Pat
  Best Thing of All.(B) 1990 (ip)

GREECE See also ANCIENT GREECE

FENTON, Edward
  Morning of the Gods.(E) 1987 (ip)
  Refugee Summer.(E) 1982 (ip)

GREYHOUND RACING

KILNER, Geoffrey
  Jet, a Gift to the Family.(E) 1979 (ip)

GRIFFINS

LYONS, Greg
  Tam's Griffin.(C) 1990 (ip)

GROWING UP See ADOLESCENCE

GROWTH

MORGAN, Alison
  Bright-eye.(C) 1985 (ip)
PATRICK, Eleanor
  Splat!(B) 1991 (ip)
WEBB, Diana
  Monster Pot-plant.(B) 1991 (ip)
WRIGHT, Gilli
  Green Fingers.(C) 1989 (op)

GUERNSEY

TREASE, Geoffrey
  Tomorrow is a Stranger.(D) 1989 (ip)
WOODFORD, Peggy
  Out of the Sun.(E) 1990 (ip)

GUIDES

SYKES, Pamela
  Juliet Joins the Guides.(D) 1986 (op)

GUILT

FOX, Paula
  One-eyed Cat.(E) 1988 (op)
HAMILTON, Virginia
  Cousins.(D) 1990 (ip)

GUINEA PIGS

EYLES, Heather
  Herbert Saves the Day.(B) 1991 (ip)
KING-SMITH, Dick
  Jenius.(D) 1990 (ip)
LEWIS, Sian
  Saddlebag Hero.(C) 1990 (ip)
WILSON, A.N.
  Hazel the Guinea-pig.(C) 1989 (ip)

GYMNASTICS

AYKROYD, Peter
  Gymnast Gilly the Champ.(E) 1988 (ip)
  Gymnast Gilly the Dancer.(E) 1986 (op)
  Gymnast Gilly the Novice.(E) 1986 (op)
DARKE, Marjorie
  Come-back.(E) 1988 (ip)
HAIGH, Sheila
  Little Gymnast.(C) 1990 (op)
  Somersaults.(C/D) 1987 (ip)

GYPSIES See TRAVELLING PEOPLE

HABITATS

DEJONG, Meindert
  Wheel on the School.(C/D) n.d. (ip)

HALLOWE'EN

BAYLIS, Jean
  Henry's Halloween.(C) 1989 (ip)

GODDEN, Rumer
  Mr McFadden's Halloween.(D) 1991
  (ip)

HAMSTERS

AKINYEMI, Rowena
  Hamster Weekend.(B) 1991 (ip)
BANKS, Lynne Reid
  I, Houdini: The Autobiography of a
  Self-educated Hamster.(D/E) 1978
  (ip)
LAVELLE, Sheila
  Harry's Hamster.(B) 1990 (ip)

HARES

HAMLEY, Dennis
  Hare's Choice.(D) 1988 (ip)
PITCHER, Diana
  Mischief Maker: African Tales of
  Nogwaya the Hare.(D/E) 1984 (op)

HEDGEHOGS

KING-SMITH, Dick
  Hodgeheg.(C) 1987 (ip)
KNIGHT, Frances
  Jasper Hedgehog Meets the
  Major.(D) 1986 (ip)
LAWHEAD, Stephen
  Tale of Anabelle Hedgehog.(C) 1990
  (ip)
PILLING, Ann
  Beast in the Basement.(C) 1988 (ip)
REDHEAD, Janet Slater
  Pins and Needles.(D) 1990 (op)

HENS AND CHICKENS

KING-SMITH, Dick
  Fox Busters.(C/D) 1980 (ip)
TOMLINSON, Jill
  Hen Who Wouldn't Give Up.(C) 1991
  (ip)

HICCUPS

POWLING, Chris
  Hiccup Harry.(C) 1988 (ip)

HIGHWAY MEN

KING-SMITH, Dick
  Toby Man.(D) 1989 (ip)

HIPPOCRATES

SMITH, Joan
  Apollo's Child.(E) 1989 (ip)

HIROSHIMA See NUCLEAR DEBATE

HISTORY See INDIVIDUAL HISTORICAL PERIODS

HOLIDAYS

LAVELLE, Sheila
  Holiday with the Fiend.(C/D) 1986
  (ip)
  Ursula by the Sea.(B) 1986 (ip)
MILLER, Moira
  Where Does Andy Go?(C) 1987 (op)
RYAN, Margaret
  Queen Bea on Holiday.(C) 1991 (ip)

HOLLAND

DEJONG, Meindert
  Journey from Peppermint
  Street.(D/E) 1975 (ip)

HOMELESSNESS

HAHN, Mary Downing
  December Stillness.(E) 1990 (ip)
STRACHAN, Ian
  Throwaways.(D/E) 1992 (ip)
URE, Jean
  Other Side of the Fence.(E) 1988 (ip)
VOIGT, Cynthia
  Homecoming.(E) 1984 (ip)

HOMOSEXUALITY

BRANFIELD, John
  Thin Ice.(E) 1983 (ip)

HONG KONG

KAYE, Geraldine
  Day after Yesterday.(D) 1981 (ip)

HORSES AND PONIES

AKRILL, Caroline
  Eventer's Dream.(D/E) 1990 (ip)
  Flying Changes.(D/E) 1985 (op)
BAGNOLD, Enid
  National Velvet.(E) 1992 (ip)

BEALE, Valerie
Emma and Freckles.(E) 1990 (ip)
CREBBIN, June
Ride to the Rescue.(C) 1989 (ip)
DICKENS, Monica
Follyfoot.(D/E) 1992 (ip)
Stranger at Follyfoot.(D/E) 1992 (ip)
DOUTHWAITE, Wendy
Orange Pony.(D) 1989 (ip)
FENNER, Carol
Summer of Horses.(D/E) 1990 (op)
GALLIER, Susan
One of the Lads: Racing on the
Inside.(E) 1988 (op)
GREAVES, Margaret
Juniper's Journey.(C) 1990 (ip)
HARDCASTLE, Michael
Saturday Horse.(D) 1990 (ip)
Switch Horse.(D) 1990 (ip)
LAVELLE, Sheila
Strawberry Jam Pony.(C) 1987 (ip)
LYTTLE, Rita
Pony Madness.(D) 1987 (op)
MANNING-SANDERS, Ruth
Book of Magic Horses.(D) 1984 (ip)
MAUGHAN, Jill
Deceivers.(D) 1990 (ip)
MORPURGO, Michael
War Horse.(D/E) 1990 (ip)
O'HARA, Mary
Catch Colt.(D/E) 1979 (ip)
My Friend Flicka.(D/E) 1989 (op)
Thunderhead.(D/E) 1974 (ip)
PEYTON, Kathleen M.
Darkling.(E) 1989 (ip)
Fly-by-night.(D) 1981 (ip)
Poor Badger.(C) 1991 (ip)
Team.(D) 1982 (ip)
ST. JOHN, Chris
Golden Girl.(D/E) 1990 (ip)
Horse of Her Own.(D/E) 1990 (ip)
Kate's Challenge.(D/E) 1990 (ip)
Riding High.(D/E) 1990 (ip)
STEINBECK, John
Red Pony.(D) 1976 (ip)
STRANGER, Joyce
Midnight Magic.(D) 1991 (ip)
TSCHIFFELY, A.F.
Tale of Two Horses.(D/E) 1989 (ip)
WILLARD, Barbara
Penny Pony.(C) 1971 (ip)

WYNNE, Elizabeth
Heronsway Series.(D) 1989 (ip)
YEATMAN, Linda
Pickles.(C/D) 1986 (ip)

HOT AIR BALLOONS

RUSH, Peter
Balloonatics.(D) 1983 (op)

HOUSES AND HOMES See also MOVING HOUSE

HUTCHINS, Pat
House That Sailed Away.(C/D) 1976
(ip)
LIVELY, Penelope
House Inside Out.(C/D) 1987 (ip)

HUMAN RIGHTS See SPECIFIC ISSUES

HUNGARY – FOLK TALES

CALVINO, Italo
Hungarian Folk Tales.(E) 1975 (ip)

HURRICANES

SALKEY, Andrew
Hurricane.(E) 1979 (ip)

HYPNOTISM

ROBSON, Denny
Great Aunt Izzy Disaster.(C) 1990
(ip)

ICE AGE

BRENNAN, J.H.
Crone.(E) 1990 (ip)

ICE SKATING

DANIEL, Mark
In a Spin.(E) 1988 (ip)
MUMMA, Barbara J.
Breaking the Ice.(D/E) 1989 (op)
Face the Music.(D/E) 1988 (ip)
Winner's Waltz.(D/E) 1989 (op)
ROSS, Mary
Ice Dancer Series.(D/E) 1990 (ip)
Robyn in a Spin.(D/E) 1991 (ip)
Robyn's Skating Challenge.(D/E)
1990 (ip)

STREATFEILD, Noel
  White Boots.(E) n.d. (ip)
WALKER, Nicholas
  Ice Mountain.(D/E) 1988 (ip)

ILLNESS See INDIVIDUAL ILLNESSES

IMAGINARY FRIENDS

BARRETT, Anne
  Midway.(D) 1985 (op)

IMMIGRANTS

COOKE, Trish
  Mammy, Sugar Falling Down.(C) 1990 (ip)
ROSEN, Billi
  Other Side of the Mountain.(E) 1990 (ip)
ROWLANDS, Avril
  Milk and Honey.(E) 1989 (ip)
SMUCKER, Barbara Claassen
  Days of Terror.(D/E) 1981 (op)

IMPS

BRADMAN, Tony
  Bub.(D) 1988 (ip)

INDIA

BOND, Ruskin
  Cricket for the Crocodile.(C) 1986 (ip)
  Dust on the Mountain.(D) 1990 (ip)
  Earthquake.(D) 1989 (ip)
  Flames in the Forest.(C) 1988 (ip)
  Getting Granny's Glasses.(C) 1985 (ip)
  Ghost Trouble.(C) 1989 (ip)
  Road to the Bazaar.(C/D) 1991 (ip)
  Snake Trouble.(C) 1990 (ip)
BOSSE, Malcolm J.
  Ganesh.(E) 1990 (ip)
BURKS, Alice Rowe
  Leela and the Leopard Hunt.(D) 1983 (op)
DESAI, Anita
  Village by the Sea.(E) 1992 (ip)
DHONDY, Farrukh
  Poona Company.(E) 1985 (ip)

GAVIN, Jamila
  Singing Bowles.(E) 1989 (ip)
POTTER, Margaret
  Boys Who Disappeared.(E) 1986 (op)
SLOAN, Carolyn
  Elephant for Muthu.(D) 1986 (ip)
SMITH, Alexander McCall
  Film Boy.(C) 1989 (ip)

INDIA – FOLK TALES

BOND, Ruskin
  Tales and legends from India.(D/E) 1982 (op)
CROUCH, Marcus
  Ivory City.(D) 1980 (ip)
GAVIN, Jamila
  Three Indian Princesses: The Stories of Savitri, Damayanti and Sita.(D) 1987 (ip)
GRAY, J. E. B.
  Indian Tales and Legends.(D/E) 1961 (ip)
SINGH, Rani
  Indian Storybook.(C/D) 1984 (ip)

INDIA – MYTHS AND LEGENDS

BOND, Ruskin
  Tales and legends from India.(D/E) 1982 (op)
JAFFREY, Madhur
  Seasons of Splendour.(D) 1985 (ip)

INDUSTRIAL REVOLUTION

GARFIELD, Leon
  Six Apprentices.(D/E) 1984 (ip)
WALSH, Jill Paton
  Chance Child.(D/E) 1985 (ip)

INDUSTRY See also CHILDREN IN INDUSTRY

WISEMAN, David
  Fate of Jeremy Visick.(D) 1984 (ip)

INUIT

GEORGE, Jean Craighead
  Julie of the Wolves.(D/E) 1972 (ip)
PAULSEN, Gary
  Dogsong.(D) 1991 (ip)

INVENTIONS

FIRMIN, Peter
Nina's Machines.(C) 1988 (ip)
SADDLER, Allen
Jerry and the Inventions.(D) 1988 (ip)

INVISIBILITY

CORMIER, Robert
Fade.(E) 1988 (ip)
CRESSWELL, Helen
Almost Goodbye Guzzler.(C) 1990
(ip)

IRELAND See also NORTHERN IRELAND

CONLAN-MCKENNA, M.
Under the Hawthorn Tree.(D/E) 1990
(ip)
KAVANAGH, P.J.
Scarf Jack.(E) 1980 (ip)
LANGENUS, Ron
Mission West.(E) 1990 (ip)
LUTZEIER, Elizabeth
Coldest Winter.(E) 1991 (ip)
LYNCH, Patricia
Turf-cutter's Donkey.(D) 1984 (ip)
MACKEN, Walter
Flight of the Doves.(D/E) 1971 (ip)
MORPURGO, Michael
Twist of Gold.(D/E) 1991 (ip)
MULLEN, Michael
Long March.(E) 1991 (ip)

IRELAND – FOLK TALES

CROKER, Thomas Crofton
Irish Folk Stories for Children.(D)
1983 (ip)
CROSSLEY-HOLLAND, Kevin
British and Irish Folk Tales.(C/D)
1990 (ip)
DEVLIN, Polly
Far Side of the Lough: Stories from
an Irish Childhood.(D) 1983 (ip)
GREGORY, Lady Augusta
Irish Legends for Children.(D) 1983
(ip)
KELLY, Eamon
Bridge of Feathers.(D) 1989 (ip)
O'BRIEN, Edna
Tales for the Telling.(C/D) 1992 (ip)

O'CONNER, Ulick
Irish Tales and Sagas.(E) 1985 (ip)
O'SHEA, Pat
Finn MacCool and the Small Men of
Deeds.(C/D) 1987 (ip)
RYAN, Jean
Land of Tales: Stories of Ireland for
Children.(C/D) 1982 (ip)
SCOTT, Michael
Tales from the Land of Erin. (3 vol-
umes).(D) 1985 (ip)
SWIFT, Carolyn
Irish Myths and Tales for Young
People.(D) 1990 (ip)
YEATS, W.B.
Fairy Tales of Ireland.(C/D) 1990 (ip)

IRON AGE

DUNDROW, Michael
Adventure on the Knolls: A Story of
Iron Age Britain.(D) 1990 (ip)
SUTCLIFF, Rosemary
Song for a Dark Queen.(E) 1984 (ip)
Sun Horse, Moon Horse.(E) 1991 (ip)

ISLANDS

TOWNSEND, John Rowe
Islanders.(E) 1981 (ip)
Rob's Place.(E) 1988 (op)

ISOLATION

HAMILTON, Virginia
Planet of Junior Brown.(E) 1987 (ip)

ISRAEL

BANKS, Lynne Reid
One More River.(E) 1973 (ip)

ITALY

MOLLOY, Anne
Christmas Rocket.(C) 1983 (op)

ITALY – FOLK TALES

CALVINO, Italo
Italian Folk Tales.(E) 1976 (ip)

JACOBITES

SUTCLIFF, Rosemary
Bonnie Dundee.(E) 1985 (ip)

JAMAICA

BARTHOLOMEW, John
 King Fernando.(C) 1986 (ip)
BERRY, James
 Future-telling Lady.(E) 1991 (ip)
 Thief in the Village and Other
 Stories.(E) 1987 (ip)
SALKEY, Andrew
 Hurricane.(D) 1977 (ip)

JAPAN

PATERSON, Katherine
 Of Nightingales that Weep.(E) 1974
 (ip)

JAPAN – FOLK TALES

MCALPINE, Helen
 Japanese Tales and Legends.(D/E)
 1989 (ip)

JEALOUSY

COCKETT, Mary
 Bickering Bridesmaids.(C) 1991 (ip)
JARMAN, Julia
 Nancy Pocket and the Kidnappers.(C)
 1991 (ip)
KLEIN, Robin
 Hating Alison Ashley.(D) 1984 (ip)
MENEZES, Anne De
 Orange Cake for Tea.(C) 1990 (ip)

JEWS

ALMAGOR, Gila
 Summer of Aviya.(E) 1991 (ip)
GERAS, Adele
 Voyage.(E) 1985 (ip)
GREENE, Bette
 Summer of my German Soldier.(E)
 1988 (ip)
HAUTZIG, Esther
 Endless Steppe.(E) 1973 (ip)
KOEHN, Ilse
 Mischling – Second Degree: My
 Childhood in Nazi Germany.(E) 1989
 (ip)
LAIRD, Christa
 Shadow of the Wall.(E) 1990 (ip)
ORLEV, Uri
 Island on Bird Street.(D/E) 1985 (op)
REISS, Johanna
 Upstairs Room.(E) 1979 (ip)

RHUE, Morton
 Wave.(E) 1988 (ip)
RICHTER, Hans Peter
 Friedrich.(E) 1978 (ip)
 I was there.(E) 1987 (ip)
ROSOFSKY, Iris
 Miriam.(E) 1990 (ip)

JEWS – FOLK TALES

ROSEN, Michael
 Golem of Old Prague.(D) 1990 (ip)
SINGER, Isaac Bashevis
 Golem.(D) 1982 (ip)
 Joseph and Koza C) 1984 (ip)
 Naftali the Storyteller and His Horse,
 Sus.(C/D) 1989 (ip)
 Stories for Children.(D) 1987 (ip)
 When Shlemiel Went to Warsaw and
 Other Stories.(C/D) 1988 (ip)

JOBS See INDIVIDUAL OCCUPATIONS

JOURNEYS See also EVACUEES, MIGRATION, REFUGEES

CONLAN-MCKENNA, M.
 Under the Hawthorn Tree.(D/E) 1990
 (ip)
DE ROO, Anne
 Traveller.(E) 1979 (ip)
GERAS, Adele
 Voyage.(E) 1989 (ip)
LIVELY, Penelope
 Voyage of QV66.(D) 1992 (ip)
LOEFF, A.Rutgers Van Der
 Children on the Oregon Trail.(D/E)
 1970 (ip)
MACKEN, Walter
 Flight of the Doves.(D/E) 1991 (ip)
MORPURGO, Michael
 Twist of Gold.(D/E) 1991 (ip)
MORRIS, Jean
 Donkey's Crusade.(E) 1989 (op)
PEYTON, Kathleen M.
 Going Home.(D) 1982 (ip)
PILLING, Ann
 Stan.(E) 1988 (ip)
PRINCE, Alison
 How's Business?(D) 1987 (ip)
SERRAILLIER, Ian
 Silver Sword.(D) 1970 (ip)

TOWNSEND, John Rowe
Golden Journey.(D/E) 1990 (op)
TREECE, Henry
Children's Crusade.(D/E) 1970 (ip)
WALSH, Jill Paton
Lost and Found.(C) 1984 (ip)

KANGAROOS

BERNARD, Patricia
Kangaroos Kids.(D) 1989 (ip)

KARATE

STRONG, Jeremy
Karate Princess.(D) 1989 (ip)
Karate Princess to the Rescue.(D) 1991 (ip)
WALKER, Nicholas
Black Belt.(D/E) 1989 (ip)

KELPIES

HUNTER, Mollie
Kelpie's Pearls.(D) 1988 (ip)
MAYNE, William
Kelpie.(D) 1987 (ip)
NIMMO, Jenny
Ultramarine.(E) 1990 (ip)

KIBBUTZ

BANKS, Lynne Reid
One More River.(E) 1988 (ip)

KIDNAPPING

CROSS, Gillian
On the Edge.(D/E) 1987 (ip)
DILLON, Eilis
Island of Ghosts.(E) 1990 (ip)
DUFFY, James
Missing.(E) 1989 (ip)
EHRLICH, Amy
Where it Stops, Nobody Knows.(E) 1989 (ip)
GILLHAM, Bill
Nothing Ever Happens Here.(D) 1990 (ip)
Rich Kid.(D) 1984 (ip)
HOLM, Anne
Hostage.(D/E) 1990 (ip)
NEWTH, Mette
Abduction.(E) 1989 (ip)

PEYTON, Kathleen M.
Prove Yourself a Hero.(E) 1988 (ip)
TREMAIN, Rose
Journey to the Volcano.(D) 1988 (ip)

KINDER SCOUT TRESPASS

SAMPSON, Fay
Free Man on Sunday.(D/E) 1987 (ip)

KING ARTHUR

BEVAN, Clare
Mightier Than the Sword.(D) 1991 (ip)
HALL, Willis
Dragon Days.(D) 1991 (ip)
PHILLIP, Neil
Tale of Sir Gawain.(D/E) 1987 (ip)
SUTCLIFF, Rosemary
Light Beyond the Forest: Quest for the Holy Grail.(D/E) 1992 (ip)
Road to Camlann.(D/E) 1984 (ip)
Sword and the Circle: King Arthur and the Knights of the Round Table.(E) 1992 (ip)
YEATMAN, Linda
King Arthur and the Knights of the Round Table.(D) 1991 (ip)

KNIGHTS

KING-SMITH, Dick
Tumbleweed.(D) 1987 (ip)
SANCHA, Sheila
Knight After Knight.(D) 1991 (ip)

LANDSCAPE

WALSH, Jill Paton
Lost and Found.(C) 1984 (ip)

LEAD MINING

GATES, Susan P.
Burnhope Wheel.(E) 1989 (ip)

LEGENDS See MYTHS AND LEGENDS

LEPRECHAUNS See FAIRY PEOPLE

LIBRARIES

FORSYTH, Anne
  Library Monster.(C) 1988 (ip)
PINTO, Jacqueline
  School Library Disaster.(C) 1986 (op)

LIGHT

LUNN, Janet
  One Hundred Shining Candles.(B) 1991 (ip)

LIGHTHOUSES

JOY, Margaret
  Little Lighthouse Keeper.(C) 1988 (ip)

LIONS

MORPURGO, Michael
  Tom's Sausage Lion.(C/D) 1987 (ip)

LIVERPOOL

SHERRY, Sylvia
  Pair of Desert Wellies.(E) 1986 (ip)
  Pair of Jesus Boots.(E) 1973 (ip)
  Rocky and the Ratman.(E) 1988 (op)

LOCAL HISTORY

ALLAN, Mabel
  Esther Crumble Lane Adventure.(E) 1983 (ip)
MARK, Jan
  Under the Autumn Garden.(D) 1980 (ip)
REES, David
  House That Moved.(C) 1982 (ip)

LOCH NESS MONSTER

BRUMPTON, Keith
  Look Out, Loch Ness Monster.(C/D) 1992 (ip)

LOGGING

WHEATLEY, Nadia
  Blooding.(E) 1987 (ip)

LOLLIPOP LADIES

WEBB, Diana
  Lily Loses Her Lollipop.(C) 1986 (op)
  Lily the Lollipop Lady.(C) 1984 (op)
  Lily's Lollipop Wand.(C) 1988 (ip)

WILLIAMS, Ursula Moray
  Bellabelinda and the No-good Angel.(D) 1982 (ip)

LONDON

ASHLEY, Bernard
  Running Scared.(D/E) 1986 (ip)
STORR, Catherine
  Underground Conspiracy.(E) 1989 (ip)
WALSH, Jill Paton
  Fireweed.(D/E) 1972 (ip)

LONELINESS

KEMP, Gene
  Gowie Corby Plays Chicken.(D) 1981 (ip)
KORALEK, Jenny
  Message in a Bottle.(D) 1987 (ip)
RYLANT, Cynthia
  Silver Packages and Other Stories.(C/D) 1987 (ip)
STORR, Catherine
  Boy and the Swan.(D) 1990 (ip)
TALBERT, Marc
  Thin Ice.(E) 1989 (ip)

LYING

ALCOCK, Vivien
  Stonewalkers.(D) 1982 (op)
ASHLEY, Bernard
  Linda's Lie.(C) 1982 (ip)
STRONG, Jeremy
  Liar, Liar, Pants on Fire!(C) 1988 (ip)

MACHINES

SMITH, Alexander McCall
  Jeffrey's Joke Machine.(C/D) 1990 (ip)
STRONG, Jeremy
  Everything Machine.(B) 1991 (ip)
  Fatbag.(C) 1983 (ip)

MAGIC

ARKLE, Phyllis
  Magic at Midnight.(C) 1974 (ip)
  Magic in the Air.(C) 1980 (ip)
BALL, Brian
  Quest for Queenie.(C) 1988 (ip)

BEACHCROFT, Nina
  Under the Enchanter.(D) 1991 (ip)
BRANFORD, Henrietta
  Royal Blunder.(C) 1990 (ip)
BURNETT, Frances Hodgson
  Secret Garden.(E) 1992 (ip)
CASSEDY, Sylvia
  Behind the Attic Wall.(D) 1987 (op)
CLEVELAND-PECK, Patricia
  Community Magic.(C) 1985 (op)
CORLETT, William
  Steps Up the Chimney.(E) 1990 (ip)
DALTON, Annie
  Witch Rose.(C) 1991 (ip)
FISHER, Catherine
  Conjuror's Game.(D) 1990 (ip)
  Fintan's Tower.(D) 1991 (ip)
FORWARD, Toby
  Storm Magic.(C) 1991 (ip)
HUNTER, Mollie
  Enchanted Whistle.(D/E) 1968 (ip)
HUTCHINS, Hazel
  Three and Many Wishes of Jason
  Reid.(D) 1987 (ip)
KORALEK, Jenny
  Knights of Hawthorn Crescent.(C)
  1986 (ip)
MANNING-SANDERS, Ruth
  Book of Enchantments and
  Curses.(D) 1976 (ip)
  Book of Magic Horses.(D) 1984 (op)
  Tales of Magic and Mystery.(D) 1985
  (ip)
MATTHEWS, Andrew
  Mallory Cox and His Magic Socks.(C)
  1990 (ip)
  Summer Witching.(C/D) 1990 (ip)
MORSE, Brian
  James' Marvellous Magic.(C) 1990
  (ip)
NIMMO, Jenny
  Snow Spider.(D/E) 1990 (ip)
  Tatty Apple.(D) 1990 (ip)
RICHEMONT, Enid
  Magic Skateboard.(D) 1991 (ip)
ROGERS, Margaret
  Cindy and the Silver Enchantress.(D)
  1982 (op)
SMITH, Alexander McCall
  Mike's Magic Seeds.(C) 1988 (ip)
  Suzy Magician.(C) 1990 (ip)

WATTS, Marjorie-Ann
  Simon the Magician.(D) 1990 (ip)

MAORIS

DE ROO, Anne
  Bat's Nest.(E) 1986 (ip)
  Jacky Nobody.(E) 1983 (ip)

MATHS

WARDLE, Terry
  Hardest Sum in the World.(D) 1986
  (ip)

MAZES

MORRIS, Jean
  Troy Game.(E) 1989 (ip)

MEASLES

POWLING, Chris
  Harry with Spots on.(D) 1990 (ip)

MEDICAL RESEARCH

CORMIER, Robert
  Bumblebee Flies Anyway.(E) 1983
  (ip)

MENTAL ILLNESS

ASHLEY, Bernard
  Dodgem.(E) 1983 (ip)
DONNELLY, E.
  Odd Stockings.(D) 1982 (ip)
FINE, Anne
  Stone Menagerie.(E) 1991 (ip)
FOX, Paula
  In a Place of Danger.(D) 1989 (ip)

MENTALLY HANDICAPPED

BYARS, Betsy
  Summer of the Swans.(D/E) 1984 (ip)
CASSEDY, Sylvia
  Me and Morton.(E) 1989 (op)
CURTIS, Philip
  Party for Lester.(D) 1984 (ip)
GILLHAM, Bill
  My Brother, Barry.(D) 1981 (ip)
HERSOM, Kathleen
  Half Child.(D/E) 1989 (ip)
KLEIN, Robin
  Boss of the Pool.(D) 1989 (ip)

LAIRD, Elizabeth
  Red Sky in the Morning.(D/E) 1988
  (ip)
MATHIAS, Beverley
  Spell Singer, and Other Stories.(D)
  1989 (ip)
MAYNE, William
  Gideon Ahoy!(D/E) 1987 (ip)
SHYER, M. F.
  Welcome Home, Jelly-Bean.(D/E)
  1982 (ip)

MERMAIDS AND MERMEN

BRANDRETH, Gyles
  Mermaid at No.13.(C) 1989 (ip)
HUNTER, Mollie
  Mermaid Summer.(D) 1990 (ip)
TOMLINSON, Theresa
  Water Cat.(D) 1989 (ip)

METALS

CHRISTOPHER, John
  City of Gold and Lead.(E) 1984 (ip)
HUGHES, Ted
  Iron Man: A Story in Five Nights.
  (C/D/E) 1985 (ip)
LIVELY, Penelope
  Astercote.(D) 1970 (ip)
O'BRIEN, Robert C.
  Silver Crown.(D) 1973 (ip)
SUTCLIFF, Rosemary
  Sun Horse, Moon Horse.(E) 1991 (ip)

MICE

ALLEN, Linda
  Meeko and Mirabel.(B) 1985 (ip)
ASCH, Frank
  Pearl's Pirates.(C) 1984 (ip)
  Pearl's Promise.(C) 1988 (ip)
CORBETT, W.J.
  Pentecost and the Chosen One.(D)
  1984 (ip)
  Pentecost of Lickey Top.(D) 1987 (ip)
  Song of Pentecost.(D) 1982 (ip)
GORDON, Margaret
  Willie Whiskers.(B) 1989 (ip)
KEMP, Gene
  Gowie Corby Plays Chicken.(D) 1981
  (ip)

KING-SMITH, Dick
  Magnus Powermouse.(C/D) 1982 (ip)
  Martin's Mice.(C/D) 1989 (ip)
MACBETH, George
  Rectory Mice.(D/E) 1984 (op)

MIDDLE AGES See also KNIGHTS

GREEN, Lynn
  Richard of Carrilon Castle.(D) 1990
  (ip)
MCCAUGHREAN, Geraldine
  Little Lower Than the Angels.(D/E)
  1987 (ip)

MIDDLE CHILD

BARRETT, Anne
  Midway.(D) 1985 (op)

MIDDLE EAST

SCHAMI, Rafik
  Handful of Stars.(E) 1990 (ip)

MIGRATION

HAGBRINK, Bodil
  Children from Tibet.(C) 1991 (ip)
KERVEN, Rosalind
  Legends of Journeys.(D) n.d. (op)
MCCAUGHREAN, Geraldine
  Snow Country Prince.(D) 1990 (ip)
MORPURGO, Michael
  Waiting for Anya.(D) 1991 (ip)

MILL WORKERS

PATERSON, Katherine
  Lyddie.(E) 1991 (ip)

MINI-BEASTS

IRESON, Barbara
  Creepy-crawly Stories.(C/D) 1987
  (ip)
LIVELY, Penelope
  House Inside Out.(C/D) 1989 (ip)

MINING See TYPES OF MINING

MOLES

WOMERSLEY, Connie
  Munro: The Mole Who Couldn't
  Sleep.(B) 1991 (ip)

MONEY

ESCOTT, John
  Mystery Money.(C) 1987 (op)
FARMER, Penelope
  Saturday by Seven.(C) 1990 (ip)
STRONG, Jeremy
  Money Doesn't Grow on Trees.(C/D)
  1984 (ip)

MONSTERS See also LOCH NESS MONSTER

ALCOCK, Vivien
  Stonewalkers.(D) 1982 (op)
DEARY, Terry
  Lambton Worm.(C) 1981 (op)
FORSYTH, Anne
  Library Monster.(C) 1988 (ip)
  Monster Flower Show.(C) 1987 (ip)
  Monster Monday.(C) 1983 (ip)
IMPEY, Rose
  Ankle Grabber.(C) 1989 (ip)
LACY, Susan
  Mussarat's Monster.(C) 1988 (op)
MANNING-SANDERS, Ruth
  Book of Monsters.(D) 1975 (ip)
MATTHEWS, Andrew
  Monster Hullabaloo!(C) 1990 (ip)
  Monster Nursery School.(C) 1991 (ip)
PARISH, Peggy
  No More Monsters for Me!(B) 1982
  (op)
RYAN, Margaret
  Sir Chancelot and the Horrible Howl-
  ing Monster.(C) 1991 (ip)
SADDLER, Allen
  Jerry and the Monsters.(D) 1988 (ip)
SEFTON, Catherine
  Blue Misty Monsters.(D) 1985 (ip)
SHRAPNEL, Pamela
  Freddie the Frightened and the Won-
  drous Ms. Wardrobe.(C) 1991 (ip)
SMITH, Susan
  Samantha Slade, Monster
  Sitter.(D/E) 1988 (ip)

MOROCCO – FOLK TALES

BARTON, Tony
  Storyteller of Marrakesh.(D) 1980
  (op)

MOTOCROSS RACING

HARDCASTLE, Michael
  Green Machine.(D) 1990 (ip)

MOTOR BIKES including RACING AND SCRAMBLING

HARDCASTLE, Michael
  Green Machine.(D) 1990 (ip)
  Roar to Victory.(D) 1991 (ip)
WESTALL, Robert
  Devil on the Road.(E) 1988 (ip)
  Futuretrack 5.(E) 1988 (ip)

MOVING HOUSE

GIRLING, Brough
  Dumbellina.(C) 1988 (ip)
HASSALL, Angela
  Jubilee Wood.(D/E) 1989 (ip)

MUSEUMS

ROSEN, Michael
  You're Thinking About
  Doughnuts.(D) 1987 (ip)

MUSIC See also SPECIFIC FORMS AND INSTRUMENTS

KEMP, Gene
  Charlie Lewis Plays for Time.(D)
  1986 (ip)
ROBINSON, Catherine
  Alphabet Cousins.(D) 1991 (ip)
  Lizzie's Luck.(E) 1989 (ip)
WELSH, Renate
  Paul the Musician.(C) 1985 (ip)
WILLSON, Robina Beckles
  Haunting Music.(C) 1987 (ip)

MYTHOLOGICAL CREATURES See GRIFFINS

MYTHS AND LEGENDS See also INDIVIDUAL COUNTRIES

BAILEY, John
  Gods and Men: Myths and Legends
  from the World's Religions.(E) 1981
  (op)
GREEN, Roger Lancelyn
  Book of Myths.(D/E) 1965 (ip)

HARRIS, Rosemary
  Lotus and the Grail: Legends from East to West.(D/E) 1985 (ip)
HODGES, Margaret
  If You Had a Horse.(D) 1987 (ip)
MERCER, John
  Stories of Vanishing Peoples.(E) 1981 (op)
PIROTTA, Saviour
  Storyworld.(B/C) 1988 (op)
REEVES, James
  Heroes and Monsters.(D/E) 1987 (ip)
SERRAILLIER, Ian
  Way of Danger.(C/D) 1965 (ip)

NAGASAKI See NUCLEAR DEBATE

NATIVE AMERICANS

COLLURA, Mary-Ellen Lang
  Jordy.(D/E) 1988 (ip)
MAYNE, William
  Drift.(E) 1987 (ip)

NATIVE AMERICANS – FOLK TALES

KERVEN, Rosalind
  Earth Magic, Sky Magic: North American Indian Tales.(C/D) 1991 (ip)

NATURAL DISASTERS See SPECIFIC DISASTERS

NATURE STORIES

MATHANE, Beryl
  Under the Hill – Stories from Brook Cottage.(B/C) 1988 (ip)

NAUGHTINESS

WOOD, Ann
  Rough and Tumble.(C) 1991 (ip)

NEIGHBOURS

FISK, Nicholas
  Back Yard War.(D) 1991 (ip)

NELSON

HAYES, Colin
  Boy from Burnham Thorpe: The Story of Lord Nelson.(D) 1989 (ip)

NEW GUINEA

LIVELY, Penelope
  House in Norham Gardens.(E) 1974 (ip)

NEW ZEALAND See also MAORIS

DE ROO, Anne
  Traveller.(E) 1983 (op)
DUNLOP, Beverley
  Spirits of the Lake.(E) 1989 (ip)
GEE, Maurice
  Champion.(D/E) 1990 (ip)
GIBSON, Gloria
  Mouse in the Attic.(D) 1980 (ip)

NINETEEN FIFTIES

HENDRY, Diana
  Double Vision.(E) 1990 (ip)
TOMLINSON, Theresa
  Water Cat.(D) 1989 (ip)

NINETEEN FORTIES

ANDERSON, Rachel
  Paper Faces.(E) 1991 (ip)

NINETEEN SIXTIES

BROOKS, Bruce
  Midnight Hour Encores.(E) 1986 (ip)

NINETEEN THIRTIES

ROBERTS, Doreen
  Parsons Road Bunch.(D) 1990 (op)

NINETEEN TWENTIES

ROBERTSON, Wendy
  Lizza.(E) 1988 (op)

NINETEENTH CENTURY See also VICTORIANS

ALINGTON, Gabriel
  Stars are Upside Down.(D/E) 1991 (ip)
BURTON, Hester
  Castors Away!(E) 1980 (op)
CARTER, Peter
  Black Lamp.(E) 1984 (ip)
HAYES, Rosemary
  Flight of the Mallard: A Fenland Adventure.(D) 1989 (ip)

HUNTER, Mollie
  Pistol in Greenyards.(E) 1988 (ip)
KILNER, Geoffrey
  Bright Key.(D) 1985 (op)
MCKENZIE, Helen B.
  Sassenach.(E) 1986 (ip)
MCLEAN, Allan Campbell
  Ribbon of Fire.(E) 1985 (ip)
  Sound of Trumpets.(E) 1985 (ip)
NEEDLE, Jan
  Fine Boy for Killing.(E) 1979 (ip)
PEYTON, Kathleen M.
  Right-hand Man.(E) 1983 (op)
PRICE, Susan
  Twopence a Tub.(E) 1991 (ip)
RENIER, Elizabeth
  Mail-coach Driver.(C) 1985 (ip)
  Secret Valley.(C) 1988 (ip)
SCOBIE, Pamela
  Twist of Fate.(E) 1990 (ip)
TURNER, Philip
  Devil's Nob.(D/E) 1970 (ip)
WILLARD, Barbara
  Farmer's Boy.(D) 1991 (ip)

NOAH'S ARK

KING-SMITH, Dick
  Noah's Brother.(C) 1986 (ip)

NORMAN ENGLAND

SUTCLIFF, Rosemary
  Knight's Fee.(E) 1990 (ip)

NORTH AMERICAN INDIANS See NATIVE AMERICANS

NORTHERN IRELAND

BANKS, Lynne Reid
  Maura's Angel.(D) 1990 (ip)
CARTER, Peter
  Under Goliath.(E) 1980 (ip)
LINGARD, Joan
  Across the Barricades.(E) 1970 (ip)
  Into Exile.(E) 1973 (ip)
  Twelfth Day of July.(E) 1970 (ip)
NORTH, Michael
  Mission to Ulster.(E) 1981 (ip)
O'NEILL, Joan
  Daisy Chain War.(D/E) 1990 (ip)

SEFTON, Catherine
  Frankie's Story.(E) 1988 (ip)
  Island of Strangers.(D/E) 1984 (ip)
  Starry Night.(E) 1986 (ip)
SUMNER, Finola
  Double the Boys.(D) 1990 (op)

NUCLEAR DEBATE including CND, HIROSHIMA, NAGASAKI, NUCLEAR WAR AND ITS AFTERMATH

BRIGGS, Raymond
  When the Wind Blows.(E) 1982 (ip)
FAVILLE, Barry
  Keeper.(E) 1988 (op)
FINE, Anne
  Goggle-eyes.(D/E) 1989 (ip)
LAWRENCE, Louise
  Children of the Dust.(E) 1985 (ip)
MAREK, Margaret
  Matt's Crusade.(E) 1990 (op)
O'BRIEN, Robert C.
  Z for Zachariah.(D) 1976 (ip)
PAUSEWANG, Gudrun
  Last Children.(E) 1989 (ip)
PITCHER, Caroline
  On the Wire.(D/E) 1989 (op)
PRINCE, Alison
  Others.(E) 1986 (ip)
SIEGEL, Barbara
  Firebrats.(E) 1988 (ip)
STRIEBER, Whitley
  Wolf of Shadows.(D) 1988 (ip)
SWINDELLS, Robert
  Brother in the Land.(E) 1986 (ip)
  Serpent's Tooth.(E) 1988 (ip)
WATSON, James
  Where Nobody Sees.(E) 1987 (ip)
WOODFORD, Peggy
  Monster in Our Midst.(E) 1989 (ip)

NUCLEAR ENERGY

COOPER, Clare
  Children of the Camps.(E) 1988 (op)
  Earthchange.(E) 1985 (op)

NUCLEAR WAR AND ITS AFTERMATH See NUCLEAR DEBATE

OBESITY

BLUME, Judy
  Blubber.(D/E) 1980 (ip)
PILLING, Ann
  Big Pink.(E) 1987 (ip)

OCCUPATIONS See INDIVIDUAL OCUPATIONS, (e.g. POSTMEN)

OGRES

POWLING, Chris
  Ziggy and Ice Ogre.(C) 1988 (ip)

OIL

HAMMOND, Ralph
  Black Gold on the Double
  Diamond.(E) 1953 (ip)

OLD AGE

ASHLEY, Bernard
  Bit of Give and Take.(C) 1986 (ip)
MAGORIAN, Michelle
  Goodnight Mr. Tom.(E) 1983 (ip)
MAHY, Margaret
  Memory.(E) 1987 (ip)
STRACHAN, Ian
  Moses Beech.(E) 1990 (ip)

OPEN-CAST MINING

RUFFELL, Ann
  Black-sand Miners.(C) 1985 (ip)

ORIGAMI

WEBB, Diana
  Mr Origami and the Paper Birds.(C)
  1985 (op)

ORPHANS

ANDERSON, Rachel
  War Orphan.(E) 1988 (ip)
LOCKHART-SMITH, Cara
  Parchment House.(D/E) 1989 (ip)
MEBS, Gudrun
  Sunday's Child.(D) 1984 (op)
ROBINSON, Catherine
  Alphabet Cousins.(D) 1992 (ip)

OTTERS

TOMLINSON, Jill
  Otter Who Wanted to Know.(C) 1991
  (ip)

WILLIAMSON, Henry
  Tarka the Otter.(D/E) 1982 (ip)

OWLS

CRESSWELL, Helen
  Two Hoots.(C) 1988 (ip)
LINDSAY, Gillian
  Owl in Winter.(C) 1986 (ip)
POTTS, Richard
  Tod's Owl.(D) 1982 (op)
TOMLINSON, Jill
  Owl Who Was Afraid of the Dark.(C)
  1973 (ip)

PACIFISM

DARKE, Marjorie
  Long Way to Go.(E) 1989 (ip)

PAINTINGS

FINE, Anne
  Anneli the Art Hater.(D) 1991 (ip)

PAKISTAN

DESAI, Anita
  Peacock Garden.(C) 1991 (ip)
STAPLES, Suzanne Fisher
  Daughter of the Wind.(E) 1990 (ip)

PAKISTAN – FOLK TALES

CROUCH, Marcus
  Ivory City.(D) 1981 (op)

PANTHERS

SAMPSON, Fay
  Josh's Panther.(D) 1988 (ip)

PAPUA NEW GUINEA – FOLK TALES

SOMERVILLE, Christopher
  South Sea Stories.(D/E) 1985 (op)

PARROTS

COTTON, Donald
  Bodkin Papers.(E) 1986 (op)
KING-SMITH, Dick
  Harry's Mad.(D) 1984 (ip)

PARTIES

POWLING, Chris
  Harry's Party.(C) 1989 (ip)
PRAGER, Annabelle
  Party Time for Nicky.(C) 1983 (ip)
PRINCE, Alison
  Job for Merv.(C) 1986 (ip)
TOWNSON, Hazel
  Victor's Party.(C) 1990 (ip)
WILSON, Jacqueline
  Party in the Lift.(C) 1989 (ip)

PATCHWORK

HUGHSON, Anne
  Rag Bag.(B/C) 1984 (ip)
WIGNELL, Edel
  Gift of Squares.(C) 1988 (ip)

PEN FRIENDS

CRAIG, George
  Pen Pals.(C) 1988 (ip)
CURTIS, Philip
  Pen Friend from Another
  Planet.(C/D) 1990 (ip)
FINE, Anne
  Pack of Liars.(D/E) 1988 (ip)

PENGUINS

TOMLINSON, Jill
  Penguin's Progress.(C) 1991 (ip)
WHITEHEAD, Andrew
  Eric, the First Flying Penguin.(C)
  1992 (ip)

PERFORMING FLEAS

MAY, Kara
  Lenny's Performing Pest.(B) 1988 (ip)

PETS AND DOMESTIC ANIMALS
See also INDIVIDUAL ANIMALS

CREBBIN, June
  Finders Keepers.(C) 1989 (ip)
MCBRIER, Page
  Oliver's Secret.(D) 1986 (ip)

PHYSICAL ABUSE

ADLER, C.S.
  Fly Free.(D) 1989 (op)
ASHLEY, Bernard
  Break in the Sun.(D/E) 1981 (ip)
  Sally Cinderella.(D) 1989 (ip)

BAWDEN, Nina
  Squib.(D/E) 1971 (ip)
BYARS, Betsy
  Pinballs.(E) 1980 (ip)

PHYSICAL DISABILITY

BEVAN, Clare
  Mightier Than the Sword.(D) 1989
  (ip)
COLE, Hannah
  In at the Shallow End.(E) 1990 (ip)
KNOWLES, Anne
  Stirrup and the Ground.(D/E) 1983
  (ip)
MATHIAS, Beverley
  Spell Singer, and other Stories.(D)
  1989 (ip)
MORGAN, Alison
  Raft.(C) 1988 (op)
ROWLANDS, Avril
  Letty.(D) 1984 (ip)
SOUTHALL, Ivan
  Let the Balloon Go.(D) 1990 (ip)
YEATMAN, Linda
  Pickles.(C/D) 1986 (ip)

PIANO

SUDBURY, Rodie
  Night Music.(D) 1983 (ip)

PIGEONS

CATE, Dick
  Flying Free.(D) 1975 (ip)
GRIFFITHS, Helen
  Hari's Pigeon.(D) 1982 (op)
KING-SMITH, Dick
  ESP: Eric Stanley Pigeon.(C) 1986
  (ip)
KINMONTH, Patrick
  Mr Potter's Pigeon.(D) 1991 (ip)
MARTIN, David
  Mr P – Street Pigeon.(D) 1975 (ip)
MUKERJI, Dhan Gopal
  Chitra: The Story of a Pigeon.(E)
  1989 (ip)
RUSSELL, Christopher
  Geordie Racer.(D) 1991 (ip)

PIGS

BAWDEN, Nina
  Peppermint Pig.(E) 1975 (ip)

CARRIS, Joan
  Just a Little Ham.(D) 1990 (op)
GIBBONS, Alan
  Pig.(C) 1990 (ip)
KEMP, Gene
  Prime of Tamworth Pig.(D) 1989 (ip)
  Tamworth Pig and the Litter.(D) 1990 (ip)
  Tamworth Pig Saves the Trees.(D) 1989 (ip)
KING-SMITH, Dick
  Ace.(C/D) 1990 (ip)
  Daggie Dogfoot.(C/D) 1980 (ip)
  Saddlebottom.(C/D) 1985 (ip)
  Sheep-pig.(D) 1983 (ip)
LEEUWEN, Jean Van
  Oliver and Amanda's Christmas.(B) 1991 (ip)
  Oliver, Amanda and Grandmother Pig.(B) 1989 (ip)
  Tales of Oliver Pig.(B) 1983 (op)
SEVERY, Richard
  Mystery Pig.(C/D) 1983 (ip)

PIONEERS

CONRAD, Pam
  Prairie Songs.(E) 1987 (ip)
LOEFF, A.Rutgers Van Der
  Children on the Oregon Trail.(D/E) 1970 (ip)
WILDER, Laura Ingalls
  By the Shores of Silver Lake.(D/E) 1990 (ip)
  Farmer Boy.(D/E) 1972 (ip)
  First Four Years.(D/E) 1978 (ip)
  Little House in the Big Woods.(D/E) 1970 (ip)
  Little House on the Prairie.(D/E) 1970 (ip)
  On the Banks of Plum Creek.(D/E) 1970 (ip)
  These Happy Golden Years.(D/E) 1970 (ip)

PIRATES

BRADMAN, Tony
  Bluebeards – Adventure on Skull Island.(C) 1988 (ip)
  Bluebeards – Mystery at Musket Bay.(C) 1988 (ip)
  Bluebeards – Peril at the Pirate School.(C) 1990 (ip)
  Bluebeards – Revenge at Ryan's Reef.(C) 1981 (ip)
MAHY, Margaret
  Pirate Uncle.(D) 1987 (ip)
  Pirates' Mixed Up Voyage: Dark Doings in the Thousand Islands.(D) 1983 (ip)
MATTHEWS, Andrew
  Quiet Pirate.(C) 1988 (ip)
NEWMAN, Marjorie
  Pirates and Captain Bullseye.(C) 1991 (ip)
  Pirates and the Cats.(C) 1990 (ip)
  Pirates and the Spring Cleaning.(C) 1989 (ip)
OLDER, Jules
  Jane and the Pirates.(C) 1984 (ip)
PESTUM, Jo
  Pirate on the Roof.(D) 1989 (ip)
PIROTTA, Saviour
  Pirates of Pudding Beach.(D) 1991 (ip)

PIXIES See FAIRY PEOPLE

PLAGUE See also EYAM

DOHERTY, Berlie
  Children of Winter.(D) 1985 (ip)
LIVELY, Penelope
  Astercote.(D) 1987 (ip)
URE, Jean
  Plague '99.(E) 1991 (ip)
WALSH, Jill Paton
  Parcel of Patterns.(D/E) 1989 (ip)

PLANTS

GOWAR, Mick
  Billy and the Man-eating Plant.(D) 1989 (ip)

POACHING

ANDERSON, Rachel
  Poacher's Son.(D) 1986 (ip)
DAHL, Roald
  Danny, the Champion of the World.(C/D) 1989 (ip)
KILNER, Geoffrey
  Bright Key.(D) 1985 (op)

POLAND

ORLEV, Uri
Island on Bird Street.(D/E) 1985 (op)

POLLUTION See CONSERVATION AND POLLUTION

POP MUSIC

KEANEY, Brian
Some People Never Learn.(E) 1991 (ip)

MCAFEE, Annalena
Girl Who Got to Number One.(E) 1991 (ip)

POSTMEN

MARTIN, Alex
Snow on the Stinker.(D) 1991 (ip)

POTHOLING

THIELE, Colin
Chadwick's Chimney.(D) 1980 (op)

POVERTY

MOLLOY, Anne
Christmas Rocket.(C) 1983 (op)

VASCONCELOS, Jose Mauro De
My Sweet-orange Tree.(D/E) 1983 (op)

PRAIRIES

CONRAD, Pam
Prairie Songs.(E) 1987 (ip)

PRE-SCHOOL SITUATIONS

HENDRY, Diana
Fiona Finds Her Tongue.(C) 1985 (ip)

PREGNANCY

DOHERTY, Berlie
Dear Nobody.(E) 1991 (ip)

PREMONITIONS

COBURN, Ann
Granite Beast.(E) 1991 (ip)

PRINCES AND PRINCESSES

KAYE, M.M.
Ordinary Princess.(C) 1981 (ip)

SINCLAIR-STEVENSON, Christopher
Hamish Hamilton Book of Princes.(C/D) 1964 (ip)

STILL, Kathy
Tractor Princess.(C) 1989 (ip)

STRONG, Jeremy
Karate Princess.(D) 1989 (ip)
Karate Princess to the Rescue.(D) 1991 (ip)

PRISONERS' FAMILIES

CAVE, Hugh B.
Uncharted Voyage.(E) 1989 (ip)

HINTON, Nigel
Buddy.(E) 1982 (ip)

KRAILING, Tessa
Only Miranda.(D) 1990 (ip)

NEEDLE, Jan
Thief.(D/E) 1989 (ip)

PECK, Richard
Through a Brief Darkness.(E) 1976 (ip)

PUMPKINS

PATRICK, Eleanor
Splat!(B) 1991 (ip)

PUPPETS

BOND, Michael
Caravan Puppets.(D) 1983 (ip)

PYGMY DEER

HILLMAN, A.
Salam the Mouse Deer: Wonder Stories of the Malayan Forest.(D) 1990 (ip)

RABBITS

ADAMS, Richard
Watership Down.(D/E) 1973 (ip)

CAREY, Joanna
One Rabbit.(B) 1991 (ip)

KENDALL, Sarita
Rabbit Club.(D) 1991 (ip)

LAMBERT, Thelma
Half Term Rabbit.(B) 1985 (ip)

MANNING-SANDERS, Ruth
Oh Really Rabbit!(C) 1980 (ip)
MEYNELL, Hugh
Only a Rabbit's Island.(D/E) 1991
(ip)
NIMMO, Jenny
Tatty Apple.(D) 1990 (ip)

RABIES

SHYDER, Zilpha Keatley
And Condors Danced.(E) 1989 (op)

RACIAL ATTITUDES

BLEZARD, Tracey
Mohan, Alone.(E) 1988 (ip)
CORLETT, William
Secret Line.(E) 1988 (ip)
DARKE, Marjorie
First of Midnight.(E) 1989 (ip)
GIBBONS, Alan
Whose Side are You On?(D/E) 1991
(ip)
GORDON, Sheila
Middle of Somewhere.(D/E) 1991 (ip)
Waiting for the Rain.(E) 1987 (ip)
GRAY, Nigel
Shots.(E) 1986 (ip)
HERLIHY, Dirlie
Ludie's Song.(D/E) 1990 (op)
IRWIN, Hadley
We are Mesquakie, We are One.(E)
1984 (ip)
JONES, Rhodri
Delroy is Here.(E) 1983 (ip)
Hillesden Riots.(E) 1985 (ip)
JONES, Toeckey
Skin Deep.(E) 1987 (ip)
MASTERS, Anthony
Taking Root.(E) 1988 (ip)
NAIDOO, Beverley
Chain of Fire.(D/E) 1991 (ip)
POWLING, Chris
Dracula in Sunlight.(D) 1990 (ip)
RAYMOND, Patrick
Maple Moon.(E) 1992 (ip)
ROWLANDS, Avril
Milk and Honey.(E) 1989 (ip)
ROY, Jacqueline
Soul Daddy.(E) 1990 (op)
SILVER, Norman
No Tigers in Africa.(E) 1992 (ip)

SMITH, Rukshana
Salt on the Snow.(E) 1988 (ip)
Sumitra's Story.(E) 1983 (ip)
TAYLOR, Mildred D.
Friendship, and Other Stories.(D)
1989 (ip)
Road to Memphis.(E) 1990 (ip)
Roll of Thunder, Hear My Cry.(E)
1977 (ip)
WARD, Glenyse
Wandering Girl.(E) 1988 (ip)

**RAILWAYS See TRAINS AND
RAILWAYS**

RAIN FORESTS

HILLMAN, A.
Salam the Mouse Deer: Wonder
Stories of the Malayan Forest.(D)
1990 (ip)
SCOTT, Bill
Shadows Among the Leaves.(D/E)
1984 (ip)

RAMBLING

SAMPSON, Fay
Free Man on Sunday.(D/E) 1987 (ip)

RAPE

CHICK, Sandra
Push Me, Pull Me.(E) 1987 (ip)

RATS

CONLY, Jane Leslie
Racso and the Rats of NIMH.(E) 1986
(ip)
RT, Margaret and the Rats of
NIMH.(D) 1990 (ip)
HUTCHINS, Pat
Rats!(D) 1989 (ip)
MCCUTCHEON, Elsie
Rat War.(D) 1985 (ip)
NASH, Margaret
Rat Saturday.(C) 1984 (ip)
O'BRIEN, Robert C.
Mrs Frisby and the Rats of NIMH.(D)
1972 (ip)
SEIDLER, Tor
Rat's Tale.(D) 1987 (ip)

READING

CLEARY, Beverly
Muggie Maggie.(C) 1992 (ip)
STORR, Catherine
Daljit and the Unqualified
Wizard.(C) 1989 (ip)

RECORDER

WILSON, Gina
Polly Pipes Up.(C) 1989 (ip)

REFORMATION

RHIND, Mary
Dark Shadow.(E) 1989 (ip)

REFUGEES

FENTON, Edward
Refugee Summer.(E) 1982 (ip)
GERAS, Adele
Voyage.(E) 1985 (ip)
HANNAM, Charles
Almost an Englishman.(E) 1979 (ip)
HAUTZIG, Esther
Endless Steppe.(E) 1988 (ip)
HOLM, Anne
I Am David.(D) 1965 (ip)
LAIRD, Mary
Kiss the Dust.(E) 1991 (ip)
LINGARD, Joan
Tug of War.(E) 1991 (ip)
SERRAILLIER, Ian
Silver Sword.(D/E) 1982 (ip)

RELATIONSHIPS See also SPECIFIC RELATIONSHIPS

ALLEN, Judy
Something Rare and Special.(E) 1989
(ip)
Travelling Hopefully.(E) 1987 (ip)
ASHLEY, Bernard
Bad Blood.(E) 1991 (ip)
Boat Girl.(E) 1990 (ip)
Dodgem.(E) 1989 (ip)
Down-and-out.(E) 1988 (ip)
High Pavement Blues.(E) 1983 (ip)
BAWDEN, Nina
Kept in the Dark.(E) 1982 (ip)

BLACKER, Terence
Homebird.(E) 1991 (ip)
BLUME, Judy
Starring Sally J Freedman as
Herself.(D) 1984 (ip)
Superfudge.(D) 1980 (ip)
Tales of a Fourth Grade Nothing.(D)
1979 (ip)
BRADMAN, Tony
You're Late, Dad.(E) 1991 (ip)
BRANFIELD, John
Fox in Winter.(E) 1989 (ip)
BRESLIN, Theresa
Different Directions.(E) 1991 (ip)
BRINSMEAD, Hesba Fay
Pastures of the Blue Crane.(E) 1978
(ip)
Sand Forest.(E) 1986 (op)
BYARS, Betsy
Animal, the Vegetable and John D
Jones.(E) 1992 (ip)
Glory Girl.(E) 1985 (ip)
Night Swimmers.(E) 1982 (ip)
Summer of the Swans.(E) 1984 (ip)
Two Thousand Pound Goldfish.(D)
1984 (ip)
CORLETT, William
Return to the Gate.(E) 1986 (op)
CORMIER, Robert
8 Plus 1.(E) 1988 (ip)
DAVIS, Jenny
Goodbye and Keep Cold.(E) 1988
(ip)
DRACUP, Angela
Placing.(E) 1991 (ip)
NOSTLINGER, Christine
Luke and Angela.(E) 1979 (ip)
VOIGT, Cynthia
Solitary Blue.(E) 1985 (ip)
Sons from Afar.(E) 1988 (ip)
WESTALL, Robert
Kingdom by the Sea.(D/E) 1992 (ip)

RESPONSIBILITY

ALCOCK, Vivien
Monster Garden.(D) 1992 (ip)
BANKS, Lynne Reid
Indian in the Cupboard.(D) 1991 (ip)

REVOLUTION See SPECIFIC REVOLUTIONS

RIVERS

BAILLIE, Allan
    Riverman.(D/E) 1986 (ip)
GREEN, Cliff
    Further Adventures of Riverboat
    Bill.(D) 1981 (ip)
KILWORTH, G.
    Drowners.(D/E) 1991 (ip)

ROBIN HOOD

ATTERTON, Julian
    Robin Hood and Little John.(D) 1989
    (ip)
CARPENTER, Richard
    Robin of Sherwood.(D/E) 1984 (op)
    Robin of Sherwood and the Hounds
    of Lucifer.(D/E) 1984 (ip)
    Robin of Sherwood: the Hooded
    Man.(D/E) 1986 (ip)
HAYES, Sarah
    Robin Hood.(D) 1989 (ip)

ROBOTS

BLAKE, John
    Roboskool: The Revenge.(D) 1991
    (ip)
BLAKE, Jon
    Oddly.(C) 1989 (ip)
CARTER, Diana
    Zozu the Robot.(D) 1986 (ip)
MAHY, Margaret
    Raging Robots and Unruly
    Uncles.(D) 1985 (ip)
PITT, Linda
    Metalmiss.(D) 1991 (ip)
PRINCE, Alison
    Type One Super Robot.(D) 1986 (ip)
STUTTARD, Marie
    Mr Chip in Paradise.(D) 1988 (op)
UMANSKY, Kaye
    Otto Matic.(C) 1990 (ip)
WADDELL, Martin
    Harriet and the Robot.(C) 1988 (ip)
WELDON, Fay
    Wolf the Mechanical Dog.(D) 1988
    (op)

ROCK MUSIC

CROSS, Gillian
    Chartbreak.(E) 1988 (ip)

ROLLER SKATING

MATHIAS, Beverley
    Kate's Skates.(B) 1990 (ip)

ROMAN BRITAIN

DYER, James
    Ravens, One Boy Against the Might
    of Rome.(D) 1990 (ip)
HARRIS, Sally
    Son of Rebellion: A Story of
    Boudica's Britain.(D) 1989 (ip)
ROCK, Nora
    Monkey's Perfect.(D) 1978 (ip)
SUTCLIFF, Rosemary
    Capricorn Bracelet.(D/E) 1990 (ip)
    Eagle of the Ninth.(D/E) 1977 (ip)
    Frontier Wolf.(E) 1983 (ip)
    Lantern Bearers.(D/E) 1981 (ip)
    Silver Branch.(D/E) 1980 (ip)
TREECE, Henry
    Legions of the Eagle.(D/E) 1970 (ip)
UPHAM, Linda
    Bronze Dagger.(D) 1989 (ip)

ROME See ANCIENT ROME

RUNNING

CHILDS, Rob
    Big Race.(C) 1988 (ip)
    Sandford on the Run.(D) 1981 (ip)
SADDLER, Allen
    Relay Race.(D) 1986 (ip)
VOIGT, Cynthia
    Runner.(E) 1986 (ip)

RUNNING AWAY

ASHLEY, Bernard
    Break in the Sun.(D/E) 1983 (ip)
BAWDEN, Nina
    Runaway Summer.(D/E) 1969 (ip)
CANNING, Victor
    Flight of the Grey Goose.(E) 1974
    (ip)
    Painted Tent.(E) 1979 (ip)
    Runaways.(E) 1978 (ip)
CROSS, Gillian
    Runaway.(D) 1979 (ip)
GEORGE, Jean Craighead
    My Side of the Mountain.(D/E) 1970
    (ip)

STRACHAN, Ian
Moses Beech.(E) 1983 (ip)
THOMAS, Ruth
Runaways.(D) 1987 (ip)
VOIGT, Cynthia
Homecoming.(E) 1984 (ip)

RUSSIA

POSELL, Elsa
Homecoming.(E) 1989 (ip)
TREASE, Geoffrey
Shadow Under the Sea.(E) 1991 (ip)

RUSSIA – FOLK TALES

CHANDLER, Robert
Magic Ring, and other Russian Folk
Tales.(E) 1983 (ip)
RANSOME, Arthur
Old Peter's Russian Tales.(D) 1984
(ip)
War of the Birds and the Beasts and
Other Russian Tales.(D) 1984 (ip)

RUSSIAN REVOLUTION

PLOWMAN, Stephanie
My Kingdom for a Grave.(E) 1970
(ip)
SMUCKER, Barbara Claassen
Days of Terror.(D/E) 1981 (op)
TREASE, Geoffrey
White Nights of St. Petersburg.(D/E)
1987 (op)

SAFETY

ELLIOTT, Michele
Willow Street Kids: It's Your Right
to be Safe.(C/D) 1986 (ip)

SAILING See BOATS AND BOATING

SAILING SHIPS

"AVI"
True Confessions of Charlotte
Doyle.(E) 1991 (ip)

SARK

GREAVES, Margaret
Grandmother Stone.(E) 1972 (ip)

SAXON ENGLAND

SUTCLIFF, Rosemary
Dawn Wind.(E) 1982 (ip)

SAXONS

CROSSLEY-HOLLAND, Kevin
Wulf.(D/E) 1988 (ip)
HAGUE, Linda
Saxon Superman: The Story of Here-
ward.(D) 1989 (ip)

SCANDINAVIA – FOLK TALES

JONES, Gwyn
Scandinavian Legends and Folk-
tales.(D) 1992 (ip)

SCHOOL CARETAKERS

WEBB, Diana
Bill Buckets.(B) 1990 (ip)

SCILLY ISLES

MORPURGO, Michael
When the Whales Came.(D/E) 1990
(ip)

SCOTLAND

DUNLOP, Eileen
Fox Farm.(D/E) 1987 (ip)
House on the Hill.(E) 1990 (ip)
Valley of Deer.(E) 1989 (ip)
GIFFORD, Griselda
Story of Ranald.(D) 1985 (ip)
GOWANS, Elizabeth
Shepherd's Flock.(D) 1986 (op)
HUNTER, Mollie
Enchanted Whistle.(D/E) 1985 (op)
Lothian Run.(E) 1984 (ip)
Pistol in Greenyards.(E) 1988 (ip)
Spanish Letters.(E) 1984 (ip)
Thirteenth Member.(E) 1986 (ip)
MCGREGOR, Iona
Edinburgh Reel.(E) 1986 (ip)
MCKENZIE, Helen B.
Sassenach.(E) 1986 (ip)
MILLER, Moira
Masque for a Queen.(E) 1987 (ip)
SPENCE, Alan
Its Colours They are Fine.(E) 1987
(ip)

48

SCOTLAND – FOLK TALES

CAMPBELL, Grant
  Scottish Fairy Tales.(C) 1980 (op)
CROSSLEY-HOLLAND, Kevin
  British and Irish Folk Tales.(C/D)
  1990 (ip)
MANNING-SANDERS, Ruth
  Scottish Folk Tales.(C/D) 1976 (ip)
MILLER, Moira
  Hamish and the Fairy Gifts.(C) 1990
  (ip)
  Hamish and the Wee Witch.(C) 1986
  (ip)
  Kist o'Whistles: Scottish Folk
  Tales.(C/D) 1990 (ip)
MONTGOMERIE, Norah
  Well at World's End.(C/D) 1985 (ip)
WILLIAMSON, Duncan
  Broonie, Silkies and Fairies: Trav-
  ellers' Tales.(D) 1985 (ip)

SEA

BAILLIE, Allan
  Adrift!(D) 1988 (ip)
HESLEWOOD, Juliet
  Tales of Sea and Shore.(D) 1983 (op)
NIMMO, Jenny
  Ultramarine.(E) 1992 (ip)
PAULSEN, Gary
  Voyage of the Frog.(D) 1991 (ip)

SEA FISHING

TOMLINSON, Theresa
  Flither Pickers.(D/E) 1992 (ip)

SEAGULLS

NEWMAN, Marjorie
  Knocked Out!(C) 1983 (ip)

SEALS

KERVEN, Rosalind
  Mysteries of the Seals.(D) 1989 (ip)
LLEWELLYN, Sam
  Pig in the Middle.(D/E) 1989 (ip)
MASTERS, Anthony
  Seventh Stream.(D) 1990 (ip)

SEASONS

WILLIAMS, Susan
  Lambing at Sheepfold Farm.(C/D)
  1982 (ip)
  Summer at Sheepfold Farm.(C/D)
  1983 (op)
  Winter Comes to Sheepfold
  Farm.(C/D) 1984 (ip)

SECRET SOCIETIES

ALCOCK, Vivien
  Trial of Anna Cotman.(E) 1991 (ip)

SENILE DEMENTIA

MAHY, Margaret
  Memory.(E) 1987 (ip)

SERENGETI

CAMPBELL, Eric M.
  Place of Lions.(E) 1990 (op)

SEVENTEENTH CENTURY

BRANFIELD, John
  Lanhydrock Days.(D) 1991 (ip)
LANGENUS, Ron
  Mission West.(E) 1990 (ip)
MULLEN, Michael
  Long March.(E) 1991 (ip)
WESTALL, Robert
  Devil on the Road.(E) 1988 (ip)

SEVENTH CENTURY

ATTERTON, Julian
  Fire of the Kings.(E) 1984 (ip)
FURLONG, Monica
  Wise Child.(E) 1987 (ip)

SEXUAL ABUSE

CORRIN, Ruth
  Secrets.(E) 1991 (ip)
HOWARD, Ellen
  Gillyflower.(D/E) 1989 (ip)
WACHTER, Oralee
  No More Secrets for Me.(D) 1983 (ip)

SHEEP AND SHEEP FARMING

DANN, Colin
  Ram of Sweetriver.(D) 1986 (ip)
WILLIAMS, Susan
  Lambing at Sheepfold Farm.(C/D)
  1982 (ip)
  Summer at Sheepfold Farm.(C/D)
  1983 (op)

Winter Comes to Sheepfold Farm.(C/D) 1984 (ip)

SHETLAND ISLANDS

KERVEN, Rosalind
Sea is Singing.(D) 1987 (ip)

SHIPWRECKS

AIKEN, Joan
Black Hearts in Battersea.(E) 1965 (ip)
BAILLIE, Allan
Adrift!(D) 1989 (ip)
BRUNNER, Hans
Survivors.(E) 1989 (ip)
HALL, Willis
Return of the "Antelope".(D) 1985 (ip)
NORTON, Mary
Borrowers Afloat.(D) 1970 (ip)

SHOES

WALSH, Jennifer
Mr Shy's Shoes.(C/D) 1990 (ip)

SHOPS

PHIPSON, Joan
Hide Till Daytime.(C) 1979 (ip)

SIBLING RIVALRY

MENEZES, Anne De
Orange Cake for Tea.(C) 1990 (ip)
URE, Jean
Hi There, Supermouse!(E) 1992 (ip)

SIKH STORIES

SINGH, Rani
Stories from the Sikh World.(C/D) 1987 (ip)

SIXTEENTH CENTURY

HUNTER, Mollie
Spanish Letters.(E) 1984 (ip)
Thirteenth Member.(E) 1986 (ip)
MILLER, Moira
Masque for a Queen.(E) 1987 (ip)
SUTCLIFF, Rosemary
Armourer's House.(D/E) 1983 (op)

WILLARD, Barbara
Queen of the Pharisees' Children.(D/E) 1989 (ip)

SIXTH CENTURY

ATTERTON, Julian
Last Harper.(E) 1983 (ip)
SUTCLIFF, Rosemary
Dawn Wind.(E) 1982 (ip)

SKATE-BOARDING

RICHEMONT, Enid
Magic Skateboard.(D) 1992 (ip)

SKATING See ICE SKATING, ROLLER SKATING

SKIING

PEYTON, Kathleen M.
Downhill All the Way.(D/E) 1988 (ip)

SKYE

MCLEAN, Allan Campbell
Hill of the Red Fox.(E) 1984 (ip)
Ribbon of Fire.(E) 1985 (ip)
Sound of Trumpets.(E) 1985 (ip)

SLATE QUARRYING

TURNER, Philip
Devil's Nob.(D/E) 1970 (ip)

SLAVES AND SLAVERY

CARTER, Peter
Sentinels.(E) 1980 (ip)
DARKE, Marjorie
First of Midnight.(E) 1989 (ip)
FOX, Paula
Slave Dancer.(E) 1979 (ip)
JONES, Rhodri
Slaves and Captains.(E) 1988 (ip)
KAYE, Geraldine
Breath of Fresh Air.(E) 1989 (ip)
LEESON, Robert
Maroon Boy.(E) 1982 (ip)
O'DELL, Scott
My Name is Not Angelica.(E) 1991 (ip)
SMUCKER, Barbara Claassen
Underground to Canada.(D/E) 1978 (ip)

TREVINO, Elizabeth Borton De
I, Juan de Pareja.(E) 1988 (ip)

SMELL

SEFTON, Catherine
Day the Smells Went Wrong.(B) 1988
(ip)
WOOD, John
Charlie and the Stinking Ragbags.(D)
1991 (ip)

SMUGGLERS

SUTCLIFF, Rosemary
Flame Coloured Taffeta.(E) 1986 (ip)

SNOOKER

DANIEL, Mark
On the Spot.(E) 1987 (ip)
HARDCASTLE, Michael
Lucky Break.(E) 1990 (op)
Snookered!(E) 1987 (ip)

SNOW

STROMSTEDT, Margareta
Matty in the Snow.(C) 1982 (ip)

SOUTH AFRICA

BREGIN, Elana
Magical Bicycle.(D) 1990 (ip)
GERAGHTY, Paul
Pig.(E) 1991 (ip)
GORDON, Sheila
Middle of Somewhere.(D/E) 1991 (ip)
MAARTENS, Maretha
Paper Bird.(D/E) 1992 (ip)
NAIDOO, Beverley
Chain of Fire.(D/E) 1991 (ip)
Journey to Jo'burg: A South African
Story.(D/E) 1991 (ip)
WATSON, James
No Surrender.(E) 1991 (ip)

SOUTH AMERICA See also
INDIVIDUAL COUNTRIES

TSCHIFFELY, A.F.
Tale of Two Horses.(D/E) 1989 (ip)

SPANISH ARMADA

BURTON, Hester
When Beacons Blaze.(C) 1978 (ip)

SPANISH CIVIL WAR

WATSON, James
Freedom Tree.(E) 1986 (ip)

SPIDERS

WHITE, E. B.
Charlotte's Web.(D) 1952 (ip)
WILLIAMS, Ursula Moray
Spid.(C) 1985 (ip)

SPORT See also INDIVIDUAL
SPORTS

ALLEN, Joy
Sports Day for Charlie.(B) 1990 (ip)
CHAMBERS, Aidan
Sporting Chance.(E) 1985 (ip)
MARK, Jan
Man in Motion.(E) 1989 (ip)

SQUIRRELS

BAWDEN, Nina
Keeping Henry.(D/E) 1988 (ip)
MCCABE, Eugene
Cyril: The Quest of an Orphaned
Squirrel.(D) 1986 (ip)

STANDING STONES

HUNTER, Mollie
Walking Stones.(D/E) 1991 (ip)

STEALING

KEMP, Gene
Turbulent Term of Tyke Tiler.(C/D)
1991 (ip)
NEEDLE, Jan
Thief.(D/E) 1990 (ip)

STEP-PARENTS

ALCOCK, Vivien
Kind of Thief.(D) 1991 (ip)
FINE, Anne
Goggle-eyes.(D/E) 1991 (ip)
HAHN, Mary Downing
Wait Till Helen Comes.(D) 1990 (ip)
JONES, Diana Wynne
Ogre Downstairs.(D) 1974 (ip)

LLOYD, Carole
  Shadow Man.(D) 1991 (ip)
MARK, Jan
  Trouble Half-way.(D/E) 1985 (ip)
NEWMAN, Marjorie
  Family Saturday.(C) 1987 (op)
ZABEL, Jennifer
  Under the Pudding Basin.(C) 1989
  (ip)

STONE-AGE

BALL, Brian
  Stone Age Magic.(C) 1989 (ip)
SAMPSON, Derek A.
  Grump and That Mammoth
  Again.(D) 1981 (ip)
  Grump and the Hairy Mammoth.(D)
  1989 (ip)
  Grump Goes Galumphing.(D) 1987
  (ip)
  Grump's Great Mammoth Hunt.(D)
  1989 (op)

STORMS

LORNSEN, Boy
  Will and the Storm.(B) 1985 (ip)
PULLEIN-THOMPSON, Christine
  Big Storm.(C) 1988 (ip)
SOUTHALL, Ivan
  Hills End.(D/E) 1970 (ip)

STRANGERS

ASHLEY, Bernard
  Your Guess is as Good as Mine.(C)
  1983 (ip)
FINE, Anne
  Stranger Danger.(C) 1989 (ip)

STUART PERIOD

MARRYAT, Captain
  Children of the New Forest.(E) 1978
  (ip)
MONTAGUE, Jeanne
  Lady Cavalier.(E) 1989 (op)
  Lady Cavalier Rides Out.(E) 1989
  (op)

SUFFRAGETTES

ALLAN, Mabel Esther
  Mills Down Below.(E) 1980 (op)

DARKE, Marjorie
  Question of Courage.(E) 1978 (ip)
WISEMAN, David
  Badge of Honour.(E) 1991 (ip)

SUICIDE

IRWIN, Hadley
  So Long at the Fair.(E) 1991 (ip)

SURFING

TOMLINSON, Theresa
  Riding the Waves.(D) 1990 (ip)
WINTON, Tim
  Lockie Leonard, Human
  Torpedo.(D/E) 1990 (ip)

SWANS

STORR, Catherine
  Boy and the Swan.(D) 1990 (ip)

SWIMMING

COLE, Hannah
  In at the Shallow End.(E) 1990 (ip)
CROSS, Gillian
  Swimathon!(D) 1991 (ip)
DUDER, Tessa
  Alex.(E) 1990 (ip)
  Alex in Winter.(E) 1990 (ip)
FINCH, Brian
  Good as Gold.(D) 1988 (ip)
KLEIN, Robin
  Boss of the Pool.(D) 1989 (ip)
LAMBERT, Thelma
  No Swimming for Sam.(C) 1985 (ip)
PINTO, Jacqueline
  School Gala Disaster.(C) 1985 (ip)

TEDDY BEARS

MILNE, A.A.
  House at Pooh Corner.(B/C) 1991 (ip)
  Winnie the Pooh.(B/C) 1992 (ip)
SALWAY, Lance
  Vain Teddy and Other Teddy Bear
  Stories.(B/C/D) 1985 (ip)
THEOBALDS, Prue
  Teddy Bear.(B/C) 1988 (ip)

TEETH

ALLEN, Joy
  Teeth for Charlie.(B) 1976 (ip)

JONES, Diana Wynne
  Wilkins' Tooth.(D/E) 1975 (ip)

TENNIS

HARDCASTLE, Michael
  Advantage Miss Jackson.(E) 1991 (ip)
WALKER, Nicholas
  Tie-break.(D/E) 1990 (op)

TERRORISM

CORMIER, Robert
  After the First Death.(E) 1979 (ip)
CROSS, Gillian
  Wolf.(E) 1992 (ip)
DICKINSON, Peter
  Seventh Raven.(E) 1981 (ip)
HARRIS, Rosemary
  Zed.(E) 1987 (ip)

THAILAND

HO, Minfong
  Rice without Rain.(E) 1989 (ip)

THEATRE See ACTING

TIAN AN MEN SQUARE

BAILLIE, Allan
  China Coin.(E) 1991 (ip)
BELL, William
  Forbidden City.(E) 1991 (ip)

TIME

LENEY, David
  Timepieces.(D) 1989 (ip)

TIME SHIFT

ALLAN, Mabel Esther
  Dream of Hunger Moss.(E) 1985 (ip)
  Romansgrove.(E) 1984 (ip)
BOSTON, Lucy M.
  Children of Green Knowe.(D) 1975
  (ip)
  Chimneys of Green Knowe.(D) 1976
  (ip)
  Enemy at Green Knowe.(D) 1977 (ip)
  River at Green Knowe.(D) 1976 (ip)
  Stones of Green Knowe.(D) 1979 (ip)
  Stranger at Green Knowe.(D) 1977
  (ip)

TIME TRAVEL

CLARKE, Joan
  Take Your Time.(E) 1990 (ip)
DOHERTY, Berlie
  Children of Winter.(D/E) 1986 (ip)
O'HARA, Marjorie
  Cunning Man's Glass.(D) 1990 (ip)

TOADS

KING-SMITH, Dick
  Henry Pond the Poet.(C) 1991 (op)

TOLPUDDLE MARTYRS

MOONEY, Bel
  Stove Haunting.(D/E) 1988 (ip)

TORTOISES

DAHL, Roald
  Esio Trot.(C/D) 1991 (ip)
KING-SMITH, Dick
  Lightning Fred.(C) 1985 (ip)
  Lightning Strikes Twice.(C) 1991 (ip)
MANNING-SANDERS, Ruth
  Tortoise Tales.(C) 1972 (ip)

TOYS AND DOLLS including GAMES (see also TEDDY BEARS)

AINSWORTH, Ruth
  Mysterious Baba and her Magic Cara-
  van.(B/C) 1990 (ip)
ARDIZZONE, Aingelda
  Little Girl and the Tiny Doll.(B) 1979
  (ip)
BAWDEN, Juliet
  Dolls' Tea Party.(B) 1990 (ip)
COCKETT, Mary
  Cat and the Castle.(C) 1982 (op)
GODDEN, Rumer
  Little Plum.(D) 1975 (ip)
  Miss Happiness and Miss Flower.(D)
  1971 (ip)
  Tottie: The Story of a Dolls'
  House.(D) 1983 (ip)
HAHN, Mary Downing
  Doll in the Garden.(D) 1990 (ip)

HOBAN, Russell
  Mouse and His Child.(D) 1969 (ip)
KENWARD, Jean
  Rag Dolly Anna.(C) 1979 (ip)
  Rag Dolly Anna's Circus.(C) 1987
  (ip)
  Rag Dolly Anna's Treasure Hunt.(C)
  1989 (ip)
  Three Cheers for Rag Dolly Anna.(C)
  1985 (op)
LEWIS, Naomi
  Silent Playmate.(C/D) 1991 (ip)
NORMAN, Roger
  Albion's Dream.(D/E) 1990 (ip)
RENDAL, Justine
  Child of Their Own.(D) 1992 (ip)
TAYLOR, Cora
  Doll.(D) 1987 (ip)
THOMSON, Pat
  Trouble in the Cupboard.(C) 1987
  (ip)
WADDELL, Martin
  Toymaker.(C) 1991 (ip)
WEBB, Diana
  Timothy Woolsey.(C) 1990 (ip)
WILLIAMS, Margery
  Velveteen Rabbit.(B/C) 1970 (ip)
WILLIAMS, Ursula Moray
  Adventures of the Little Wooden
  Horse.(C) 1970 (ip)
  Further Adventures of Gobbolino and
  the Little Wooden Horse.(C) 1984
  (ip)
  Gobbolino the Witch's Cat.(C) 1969
  (ip)

TRADE UNIONS

CROSS, Gillian
  Revolt at Ratcliffe's Rags.(E) 1983
  (op)
HOWKER, Janni
  Nature of the Beast.(E) 1985 (ip)
MOONEY, Bel
  Flower of Jet.(D/E) 1991 (ip)
  Stove Haunting.(D/E) 1988 (ip)

TRAINS AND RAILWAYS

CROSS, Gillian
  Iron Way.(D/E) 1979 (ip)
LAMBERT, Thelma
  No Train for Sam.(C) 1989 (ip)

MAYNE, William
  Tiger's Railway.(D) 1991 (ip)
SADDLER, Allen
  Smudger's Saturday Special.(D) 1988
  (op)
SEVERY, Richard
  Angel.(D/E) 1988 (ip)
WILLS, Jean
  Railway Computer.(C) 1983 (ip)

TRANSPLANTS

DICKINSON, Peter
  Eva.(E) 1988 (ip)

TRANSPORTATION

NICHOLSON, Joyce
  Convict's Daughter.(D/E) 1988 (ip)

TRAVELLING PEOPLE

ALLEN, Judy
  Dream Thing.(E) 1990 (ip)
GODDEN, Rumer
  Diddakoi.(D) 1991 (ip)
GRANT, Gwen
  Gypsy Racer.(D) 1991 (ip)
HUNTER, Mollie
  I'll Go My Own Way.(E) 1987 (ip)
MAYNE, William
  Winter Quarters.(E) 1982 (ip)
MCCAUGHREAN, Geraldine
  Little Lower Than the Angels.(D/E)
  1991 (ip)
ROBEY, Sally
  Tyso's Promise.(E) 1987 (ip)
RUSH, Peter
  Travellers' Tales.(D/E) 1983 (ip)
SINCLAIR, Olga
  Gypsy Girl.(C) 1981 (ip)
TAYLOR, Robert
  Line of Dunes.(D) 1984 (ip)
WILLARD, Barbara
  Queen of the Pharisees'
  Children.(D/E) 1989 (ip)
WILLIAMSON, Duncan
  Fireside Tales of the Traveller Chil-
  dren.(D) 1985 (ip)
  Genie and the Fisherman: And Other
  Tales from the Travelling People.(D)
  1991 (ip)
  Tell Me a Story for Christmas.(D)
  1989 (ip)

TRAVELLING PLAYERS

BROWN, Pamela
Family Playbill.(E) 1986 (ip)

TREASURE

MAHY, Margaret
Clancy's Cabin.(C) 1987 (ip)
NEEDLE, Jan
Losers Weepers.(D) 1981 (ip)

TREES

PHILLIPS, Ann
Oak King and the Ash Queen.(D)
1984 (ip)

TROLLS

JUNGMAN, Ann
There's a Troll at the Bottom of My
Garden.(C) 1991 (ip)
WRIGHT, Ralph
Vegetarian Troll.(C) 1992 (ip)

TRUANCY

URE, Jean
King of Spuds.(C) 1989 (ip)

TRUMPET

LINE, David
Screaming High.(E) 1987 (ip)

TUDOR PERIOD

DYMOKE, Juliet
Aboard the "Mary Rose".(E) 1985
(op)
Spanish Boy.(E) 1987 (ip)
HARNETT, Cynthia
Stars of Fortune.(E) 1981 (op)
TREASE, Geoffrey
Cue for Treason.(D/E) 1986 (ip)
WILLARD, Barbara
Mantlemass Series.(E) 1989 (ip)

TURKEY

HICYILMAZ, Gaye
Against the Storm.(E) 1990 (ip)

TWELFTH CENTURY

ATTERTON, Julian
Knights of the Lost Domain.(E) 1991
(ip)
Knights of the Sacred Blade.(E) 1989
(ip)
LAIRD, Christa
Forgotten Son.(E) 1990 (ip)
SUTCLIFF, Rosemary
Witch's Brat.(D/E) 1990 (ip)

TWENTIETH CENTURY

HOWKER, Janni
Isaac Campion.(E) 1986 (ip)

TWINS

FINE, Anne
Round Behind the Ice-house.(E) 1990
(ip)
REUTERSWARD, Maud
Noah is My Name.(B/C) 1991 (ip)

U.S.A. See UNITED STATES OF AMERICA

UFOS See UNIDENTIFIED FLYING OBJECTS

UNDERGROUND

MARK, Jan
Under the Autumn Garden.(D) 1980
(ip)

UNEMPLOYMENT

HOWKER, Janni
Nature of the Beast.(E) 1985 (ip)
JONES, Rhodri
So Far to Go.(E) 1987 (ip)

UNICORNS

DOHERTY, Berlie
Spellhorn.(D/E) 1989 (ip)
SEVERY, Richard
Unicorn Trap.(D) 1984 (ip)

UNIDENTIFIED FLYING OBJECTS

FEINSTEIN, Stephen
Out of This World.(D) 1990 (ip)
FLEETWOOD, Jenni
Intergalactic Omniglot.(D) 1989 (ip)

UNITED STATES OF AMERICA

FORBES, Esther
  Johnny Tremain.(E) 1943 (ip)

VACUUM CLEANERS

STRONG, Jeremy
  Fatbag.(C) 1983 (ip)

VAMPIRES

PERRY, Ritchie
  Fenella Fang and the Great
  Escape.(D) 1988 (op)
  Fenella Fang and the Time
  Machine.(D) 1991 (ip)
  Fenella Fang and the Wicked
  Witch.(D) 1989 (ip)
PETTERSSON, Allan Rune
  Frankenstein's Aunt.(D) 1982 (ip)
PIROTTA, Saviour
  Vampire Trees.(D) 1991 (ip)
SEYMOUR, Miranda
  Vampire of Verdonia.(D) 1987 (op)
SOMMER-BODENBURG, Angela
  Little Vampire in Love.(D) 1988 (ip)
  Little Vampire Takes a Trip.(D) 1985
  (ip)
SWINDELLS, Robert
  Dracula's Castle.(C/D) 1990 (ip)

VANDALISM

ESCOTT, John
  Orange Revenge.(D) 1990 (ip)
SCHLEE, Ann
  Vandal.(E) 1987 (ip)

VICTORIAN PERIOD

AIKEN, Joan
  Black Hearts in Battersea.(E) 1992
  (ip)
  Midnight is a Place.(D/E) 1991 (ip)
ALLAN, Mabel Esther
  Romansgrove.(E) 1984 (ip)
AVERY, Gillian
  Mouldy's Orphan.(D) 1981 (ip)
BENEDICTUS, David
  Little Sir Nicholas.(D) 1990 (ip)
BROWN, Pamela
  Family Playbill.(E) 1986 (ip)
BURNETT, Frances Hodgson
  Little Lord Fauntleroy.(E) 1984 (ip)
  Little Princess.(E) 1990 (ip)

DRAZIN, Judith
  Midsummer Picnic.(C) 1982 (ip)
GARFIELD, Leon
  Blewcoat Boy.(E) 1988 (ip)
  December Rose.(D/E) 1986 (ip)
LIVELY, Penelope
  Fanny and the Monsters.(D/E) 1983
  (ip)
  Stitch in Time.(E) 1976 (ip)
PEARCE, Philippa
  Tom's Midnight Garden.(D/E) 1989
  (ip)
PRICE, Susan
  Twopence a Tub.(E) 1991 (ip)
TOMLINSON, Theresa
  Flither Pickers.(D/E) 1992 (ip)

VIDEOS

ROSEN, Michael
  Class Two Monster.(D) 1989 (ip)

VIETNAM AND VIETNAMESE

GIBBONS, Alan
  Jaws of the Dragon.(D/E) 1991 (ip)

VIETNAM WAR

ANDERSON, Rachel
  War Orphan.(E) 1988 (ip)

VIKINGS

DILLON, Eilis
  Singing Cave.(E) 1992 (ip)
HAYES, Rosemary
  Mission from the Marsh: King Alfred
  and the Vikings.(D) 1991 (ip)
MULLEN, Michael
  Sea Wolves from the North.(D) 1983
  (ip)
SUTCLIFF, Rosemary
  Blood Feud.(E) 1978 (ip)
SWINDELLS, Robert
  Voyage to Valhalla.(D/E) 1977 (ip)
TREECE, Henry
  Horned Helmet.(D) 1970 (ip)
WALSH, Jill Paton
  Hengest's Tale.(D) 1988 (ip)

VINTAGE CARS

FISK, Nicholas
  Leadfoot.(D) 1992 (ip)

VIOLENCE

HINTON, S.E.
  Rumble Fish.(E) 1977 (ip)

VOLCANOES

TREMAIN, Rose
  Journey to the Volcano.(D) 1988 (ip)

VOLES

LAWHEAD, Stephen
  Tale of Jeremy Vole.(C) 1990 (ip)

VOYAGES See JOURNEYS

WALES

NIMMO, Jenny
  Chestnut Soldier.(D/E) 1991 (ip)
  Emlyn's Moon.(D/E) 1989 (ip)
  Snow Spider.(D/E) 1990 (ip)
TAYLOR, Robert
  Dewin.(D) 1983 (ip)
WEBB, Harri
  Tales from Wales.(D) 1984 (ip)

WALES – FOLK TALES

CROSSLEY-HOLLAND, Kevin
  British and Irish Folk Tales.(C/D)
  1990 (ip)
JONES, Gwyn
  Welsh Legends and Folk Tales.(D)
  1990 (ip)
MORRIS, Jan
  My Favourite Stories of Wales.(D)
  1980 (ip)

WALES – MYTHS AND LEGENDS

EDWARDS, John Emlyn
  Dragons of Snowdon.(C) 1989 (op)
WEBB, Harri
  Tales from Wales.(D) 1984 (ip)

WAR See also SPECIFIC WARS

DEJONG, Meindert
  House of Sixty Fathers.(D) 1988 (ip)
DICKINSON, Peter
  A.K.(E) 1990 (ip)

WASHING MACHINES

ROSEN, Michael
  Norma and the Washing
  Machine.(B/C) 1988 (ip)

WATER

MORRIS, Jean
  Song Under the Water.(E) 1985 (op)
WEBB, Beth
  Magic in the Pool of Making.(D) 1992
  (ip)

WEASELS

McBRATNEY, Sam
  Uncle Charlie Weasel's Winter.(D)
  1988 (ip)

WEATHER

LORNSEN, Boy
  Will and the Storm.(C) 1985 (ip)
PULLEIN-THOMPSON, Christine
  Big Storm.(B) 1988 (ip)
RUFFELL, Ann
  Sun and Rain.(C) 1986 (ip)
  Too Small.(C) 1987 (ip)
SALKEY, Andrew
  Hurricane.(D) 1979 (ip)
STROMSTEDT, Margareta
  Matty in the Snow.(C) 1982 (ip)

WEST INDIES See also INDIVIDUAL COUNTRIES

CHERRINGTON, Clare
  Sunshine Island Moonshine
  Baby.(C/D) 1984 (ip)
HALLWORTH, Grace
  Mouth Open, Story Jump Out.(D)
  1992 (ip)

WEST INDIES – FOLK TALES

CHARLES, Faustin
  Tales from the West Indies.(D) 1985
  (op)
BERRY, James
  Anancy – Spiderman.(D/E) 1988 (ip)
MAKHANLALL, D.
  Brer Anansi Strikes Again.(D) 1976
  (ip)
  Brer Anansi's Bag of Tricks.(D) 1978
  (ip)

Further Adventures of Brer Anansi.(D) 1980 (ip)
SALKEY, Andrew
Caribbean Folk Tales and Legends.(D/E) 1980 (ip)
SHERLOCK, Philip M.
Anancy the Spider Man.(D) 1983 (ip)
Ears and Tails and Commonsense.(D) 1983 (ip)
Iguana's Tail.(D) 1979 (ip)

WHALES

CORBETT, W.J.
Toby's Iceberg.(D) 1992 (ip)
LUCAS, Jeremy
Whale.(E) 1983 (op)
MORPURGO, Michael
When the Whales Came.(D/E) 1990 (ip)

WIND SURFING

ROSS, Mary
Window in the Sail.(D/E) 1991 (ip)

WINDMILLS

DEARY, Terry
Windmill of Nowhere.(C) 1984 (ip)

WITCHES AND WIZARDS

APPS, Roy
Twitches.(B) 1990 (ip)
Twitches Go on Horriday.(B) 1991 (ip)
BARRY, Margaret Stuart
Return of the Witch.(C) 1979 (ip)
Simon and the Witch.(C) 1992 (ip)
Witch and the Holiday Club.(C) 1988 (ip)
Witch of Monopoly Manor.(C) 1981 (ip)
Witch on Holiday.(C) 1984 (ip)
Witch VIP.(C) 1988 (ip)
BEACHCROFT, Nina
Well Met by Witchlight.(C) 1990 (ip)
BLACKER, Terence
In Control, Ms Wiz?(C) 1990 (ip)
In Stitches with Ms Wiz.(C) 1989 (ip)
Ms Wiz Banned!(C) 1990 (ip)
Ms Wiz Goes Live.(C) 1990 (ip)
Ms Wiz Spells Trouble.(C) 1988 (ip)
You're Nicked, Ms Wiz.(C) 1989 (ip)

BOON, John
Help for the High Street Witch.(C) 1987 (op)
High Street Witch at the Zoo.(C) 1988 (ip)
BYRNE, Corley
Princess and the Dragon-hamster.(D) 1985 (ip)
CASS, Joan
Witches Go on a Package Holiday.(C) 1986 (op)
CHICHESTER, Imogen
Witch-child.(D) 1985 (ip)
COOMBS, Patricia
Dorrie and the Goblin.(C) 1991 (ip)
COOPER, Clare
Wizard Called Jones.(D) 1984 (op)
CRESSWELL, Helen
Lizzie Dripping.(C) 1985 (ip)
Lizzie Dripping and the Witch.(C) 1991 (ip)
DAHL, Roald
Witches.(C/D) 1990 (ip)
EDWARDS, Dorothy
Witches and the Grinnygog.(D) 1981 (ip)
FLANAGAN, Joan
Witch's House.(D) 1991 (ip)
GEBLER, Carlo
Witch That Wasn't.(C) 1991 (ip)
JONES, Diana Wynne
Charmed Life.(E) 1979 (ip)
Witch Week.(E) 1989 (ip)
JUNGMAN, Ann
Broomstick Services.(C) 1990 (ip)
KLEIN, Robin
Broomstick Academy.(C) 1986 (ip)
MANNING-SANDERS, Ruth
Book of Sorcerers and Spells.(D) 1973 (ip)
Book of Witches.(D) 1981 (op)
MATTHEWS, Andrew
Mallory Cox and His Magic Socks.(C) 1991 (ip)
Wickedoz.(C) 1991 (ip)
MUIR, Helen
Wonderwitch.(C) 1988 (ip)
Wonderwitch and the Rooftop Cats.(C) 1991 (ip)

MURPHY, Jill
Bad Spell for the Worst Witch.(C)
1983 (ip)
Worst Witch.(C) 1978 (ip)
PEARSON, Maggie
Donnabella.(C) 1988 (ip)
POWLING, Chris
Fly-away Frankie.(C) 1987 (ip)
SLEIGH, Barbara
Broomsticks and Beasticles: Stories
and Verse About Witches and Strange
Creatures.(D) 1984 (op)
Grimblegraw and the Wuthering
Witch.(C) 1980 (op)
STOREY, Margaret
Double Wizard.(D) 1979 (ip)
STORR, Catherine
Daljit and the Unqualified
Wizard.(C) 1989 (ip)
STRONG, Jeremy
Fanny Witch and the Thunder
Lizard.(C) 1989 (ip)
UMANSKY, Kaye
Pongwiffy: A Witch of Dirty
Habits.(D) 1988 (ip)
WELFARE, Mary
Bandit Badwitch.(C) 1988 (ip)
Witchdust.(C) 1980 (ip)
WHITEHEAD, Victoria
Chimney Witch Chase.(C/D) 1987
(ip)
Chimney Witches.(C/D) 1988 (ip)
WILLSON, Robina Beckles
Holiday Witch.(C) 1983 (op)
Hungry Witch.(C) 1984 (ip)
Secret Witch.(C) 1982 (op)
Sporty Witch.(C) 1986 (op)
WRIGHT, Ralph
Witch Goes for Gold.(D) 1989 (ip)
Witch's Funny Bone.(D) 1986 (op)

WIZARDS See WITCHES AND WIZARDS

WOLVES

BURGESS, Melvin
Cry of the Wolf.(E) 1990 (ip)
JUNGMAN, Ann
Lucy and the Big Bad Wolf.(C) 1992
(ip)
Lucy and the Wolf in Sheep's Cloth-
ing.(D) 1989 (ip)

STORR, Catherine
Clever Polly and the Stupid Wolf.(C)
1967 (ip)
Polly and the Wolf Again.(C) 1970
(ip)
Tales of Polly and the Hungry
Wolf.(D) 1982 (ip)

WOMEN'S RIGHTS

CORBALIS, Judy
Wrestling Princess and Other
Stories.(C/D) 1992 (ip)
GIRLING, Brough
Vera Pratt and the False
Moustaches.(D) 1987 (ip)
SHAW, Margret
Wider Tomorrow.(E) 1989 (ip)
STAPLES, Suzanne Fisher
Daughter of the Wind.(E) 1991 (ip)

WORLD WAR I

ANDERSON, Rachel
Poacher's Son.(D) 1986 (ip)
BARBER, Antonia
Ring in the Rough Stuff.(E) 1984 (op)
COOPER, Gordon
Hour in the Morning.(E) 1971 (ip)
Time in the City.(E) 1972 (ip)
DARKE, Marjorie
Long Way to Go.(E) 1989 (ip)
Rose from Blighty.(E) 1992 (ip)
FARMER, Penelope
Charlotte Sometimes.(D) 1985 (ip)
HARRIS, John
Fledglings.(E) 1980 (op)
Victors.(E) 1980 (op)
HILL, Susan
Strange Meeting.(E) 1973 (ip)
MACBETH, George
Rectory Mice.(D/E) 1984 (op)
NEWBERY, Linda
Kind Ghosts.(E) 1991 (ip)
Some Other War.(E) 1990 (ip)
O'NEILL, Judith
Deepwater.(D/E) 1989 (op)
PEYTON, Kathleen M.
Thunder in the Sky.(D/E) 1990 (ip)
ROSTKOWSKI, Margaret
After the Dancing Days.(E) 1990 (ip)

ROWE, Alick
Voices of Danger.(E) 1992 (ip)
TREADGOLD, Mary
Journey from the Heron.(D/E) 1981 (op)
WELCH, Ronald
Tank Commander.(D/E) 1972 (ip)

WORLD WAR II See also EVACUEES

ALINGTON, Gabriel
Evacuee.(D) 1988 (ip)
ANDERSON, Rachel
Paper Faces.(E) 1991 (ip)
BAWDEN, Nina
Carrie's War.(D/E) 1992 (ip)
Keeping Henry.(D/E) 1988 (ip)
BROWN, Pamela
Finishing School.(E) 1984 (ip)
BURTON, Hester
In Spite of all Terror.(E) 1968 (ip)
COOPER, Gordon
Certain Courage.(E) 1975 (ip)
COOPER, Susan
Dawn of Fear.(D/E) 1974 (ip)
DAVIES, Andrew
Conrad's War.(D) 1980 (ip)
DICKS, Terrance
Prisoners of War.(D) 1990 (ip)
DONALDSON, Margaret
Moon's on Fire.(E) 1980 (ip)
GILLHAM, Bill
Home Before Long.(D) 1983 (ip)
HAMLEY, Dennis
War and Freddy.(D) 1991 (ip)
HANNAM, Charles
Boy in Your Situation.(E) 1988 (ip)
HAUTZIG, Esther
Endless Steppe.(E) 1988 (ip)
HEUCK, Sigrid
Hideout.(D/E) 1991 (ip)
HILL, Deirdre
Flight from Fear.(D/E) 1989 (ip)
KOEHN, Ilse
Mischling – Second Degree: My Childhood in Nazi Germany.(E) 1989 (ip)
LAIRD, Christa
Shadow of the Wall.(E) 1990 (ip)
LINGARD, Joan
Between Two Worlds.(D/E) 1991 (ip)
File on Fraulein Berg.(D/E) 1985 (ip)
Tug of War.(D/E) 1990 (ip)

LOWRY, Lois
Number the Stars.(E) 1991 (ip)
MACLACHLAN, Mairi
River Tree.(E) 1988 (op)
MAGORIAN, Michelle
Good-night Mr Tom.(D) 1983 (ip)
MORPURGO, Michael
Friend or Foe.(D) 1977 (ip)
Waiting for Anya.(D) 1991 (ip)
MUKERJI, Dhan Gopal
Chitra: The Story of a Pigeon.(E) 1989 (ip)
NOONAN, Michael
McKenzie's Boots.(D/E) 1989 (ip)
NOSTLINGER, Christine
Fly Away Home.(E) 1985 (ip)
O'NEILL, Judith
Jess and the River Kids.(D/E) 1990 (ip)
ORGEL, Doris
Devil in Vienna.(E) 1991 (ip)
ORLEV, Uri
Island on Bird Street.(D/E) 1985 (op)
PRINCE, Alison
How's Business?(D) 1989 (ip)
REISS, Johanna
Upstairs Room.(D/E) 1979 (ip)
RICHTER, Hans Peter
I Was There.(D/E) 1987 (ip)
SEREDY, Kate
Chestry Oak.(D) 1985 (op)
SERRAILLIER, Ian
Silver Sword.(D) 1982 (ip)
TREASE, Geoffrey
Arpino Assignment.(D/E) 1988 (ip)
Tomorrow is a Stranger.(D) 1989 (ip)
WALSH, Jill Paton
Dolphin Crossing.(E) 1970 (ip)
Fireweed.(E) 1972 (ip)
WESTALL, Robert
Blitzcat.(D/E) 1991 (ip)
Echoes of War.(E) 1989 (ip)
Fathom Five.(E) 1979 (ip)
Kingdom by the Sea.(D/E) 1992 (ip)
Machine-gunners.(E) 1977 (ip)
WILD, Margaret
Let the Celebrations Begin!(E) 1991 (ip)
WOODFORD, Peggy
Out of the Sun.(E) 1991 (ip)

WRECKERS

SAMPSON, Fay
    Jenny and the Wreckers.(C) 1984 (ip)

YETIS

MORPURGO, Michael
    King of the Cloud Forest.(D/E) 1989
    (ip)

YORKSHIRE

MAYNE, William
    While the Bells Ring.(D) 1979 (ip)

MORGAN, Ellen
    Another Winter's Tale.(E) 1987 (op)

ZIMBABWE – FOLK TALES

CHISIYA
    African Lullaby.(C) 1986 (ip)

ZOOS

DAHL, Tessa
    Gwenda and the Animals.(C) 1992
    (ip)
MUIR, Helen
    Tiger Trouble.(C) 1989 (op)
PILLING, Ann
    No Guns, no Oranges.(C) 1986 (ip)